ADVANCE PRAISE FOR *THE FIRST BLACK MARINES*

"Detailed, well-written, and highly accurate, *The First Black Marines* offers a model for how we should teach oral history in the twenty-first century."

REGINALD K. ELLIS *Florida A&M University*

"This graphic history walks students step-by-step through the field of history and what it means to be a historian. Stunning visuals recreate life at Montford Point for the first African American Marines since the American Revolution. *The First Black Marines* sheds light on their experiences as men, Marines, and African Americans fighting for the double victory in the Jim Crow South and in the Pacific Theater of World War II. These men faced discrimination, hardship, and injustice with poise and honor, and their stories, interpreted through the eyes of historians Trevor Getz, Robert Willis, and Master Gunnery Sergeant Joseph H. Geeter, III, provide insight into how the battle for civil rights was fought on a multitude of fronts while providing the reader with lessons that are still applicable to the struggles our country faces today."

TONI NICHOLAS *Red Rocks Community College*

"*The First Black Marines* provides a much-needed corrective to the whitewashed version of America's involvement in World War II with which many of us are all too familiar. The oral histories conducted with the Montford Marines give readers personal insights into the experiences of African Americans in the Jim Crow military. As these men share their accounts of segregation and injustice, but also the pride and meaning with which they served, readers come away with a much-needed understanding of not only their sacrifices but also their resiliency. True to form, this new entry in Oxford's excellent Graphic History Series provides a thoroughly useful historical context, interpretation, and methods discussion, as well as primary sources, to make this a perfect book for classes on US history, African American experiences, public history, and America's participation in World War II."

MARGARET B. BODEMER *California Polytechnic State University, San Luis Obispo*

THE FIRST
BLACK MARINES

THE FIRST BLACK MARINES

AN ORAL HISTORY
A GRAPHIC HISTORY

TREVOR R. GETZ

ROBERT WILLIS

JOSEPH H. GEETER III

LIZ CLARKE

OXFORD
UNIVERSITY PRESS

Oxford University Press is a department of the University of Oxford.
It furthers the University's objective of excellence in research, scholarship,
and education by publishing worldwide. Oxford is a registered trade mark
of Oxford University Press in the UK and in certain other countries.

Published in the United States of America by Oxford University Press
198 Madison Avenue, New York, NY 10016, United States of America.

© 2025 by Oxford University Press

For titles covered by Section 112 of the US Higher Education Opportunity
Act, please visit www.oup.com/us/he for the latest information about
pricing and alternate formats.

All rights reserved. No part of this publication may be reproduced,
stored in a retrieval system, or transmitted, in any form or by any means,
without the prior permission in writing of Oxford University Press,
or as expressly permitted by law, by license or under terms agreed with
the appropriate reprographics rights organization. Inquiries concerning
reproduction outside the scope of the above should be sent to the Rights
Department, Oxford University Press, at the address above.

You must not circulate this work in any other form
and you must impose this same condition on any acquirer

Library of Congress Cataloging-in-Publication Data

Names: Getz, Trevor R, author. | Willis, Robert, author. | Geeter, Joe,
 III, author. | Clarke, Liz, 1982- illustrator.
Title: The first Black Marines : an oral history, a graphic history /
 Trevor R Getz, Robert Willis, Joseph H Geeter III ; [illustrated by] Liz
 Clarke.
Description: [New York] : Oxford University Press, [2024] | Includes
 bibliographical references. | Summary: "Based on original interviews
 with World War II veterans, The First Black Marines chronicles the
 powerful stories of the first African American men who trained and
 served in the US Marine Corps during the Jim Crow era. As a highly
 accessible introduction to oral history methodology, this graphic
 history empowers students to conduct their own research projects"—
 Provided by publisher.
Identifiers: LCCN 2024021396 (print) | LCCN 2024021397 (ebook) | ISBN
 9780197650370 (paperback) | ISBN 9780197650387 (epub)
Subjects: LCSH: United States. Marine Corps—African
 Americans—History—20th century—Comic books, strips, etc. | United
 States. Marine Corps—African Americans—Biography—Comic books, strips,
 etc. | Montford Point Camp (Camp Lejeune, N.C.)—Comic books, strips,
 etc. | United States. Marine Corps—Recruiting, enlistment, etc.—World
 War, 1939–1945—Comic books, strips, etc. | World War,
 1939–1945—Participation, African American—Comic books, strips, etc. |
 Race discrimination—United States—History—20th century—Comic books,
 strips, etc.
Classification: LCC VE23 .G48 2024 (print) | LCC VE23 (ebook) | DDC
 359.9/608996073—dc23/eng/20240517
LC record available at https://lccn.loc.gov/2024021396
LC ebook record available at https://lccn.loc.gov/2024021397

Printed by Integrated Books International, United States of America

CONTENTS

List of Maps IX
Preface XI
About the Authors and the Illustrator XIII

PART I
THE GRAPHIC HISTORY — 1

Chapter 1: When I Grow Up 3
Chapter 2: Where Hell Starts 21
Chapter 3: Black Marines in Jim Crow America 33
Chapter 4: Let the Mosquitoes Eat 51
Chapter 5: All of Them Are Legendary 77
Chapter 6: A 17-Year-Old Kid with a .45 Pistol 101
Chapter 7: Aftermaths and Legacies 117

PART II
STARTING A RESEARCH PROJECT — 133

Introduction 135
Defining Questions 136
Building a Critical Bibliography 137

PART III
HISTORICAL CONTEXT — 147

Jim Crow America 149
African American and the US Military during the
   Second World War 152
Montford Point Camp and the First Black Marines 155
Montford Pointers in the Pacific Theater of Operations ... 161
The Tension of Masculinity 164
Looking Both Forward and Backward 166

VII

PART IV
ORAL HISTORY: APPLYING A RESEARCH METHODOLOGY — 171
    Oral History as Method — 173
    Oral History and Memory — 175
    Oral History as a Community Act — 178
    Our Approach and Experiences — 179

PART V
INTERPRETATION — 183
    What Is the Job of the Historian in Interpretation? — 185
    Critical Analysis — 187
    Narrative Structures and Shared Experiences — 189
    Analytical Moments: Hearing Individual Messages — 192
    Interpreting through Comics: Choices and Debates — 194

PART VI
PRIMARY SOURCES — 197
    Document 1: Executive Order 8802. Prohibition of Discrimination in the Defense Industry (1941) — 199
    Document 2: Letter of Instruction No. 421 (1943) — 200
    Document 3: *Pittsburgh Courier*, "The Courier's Double 'V' for a Double Victory Campaign Gets Country-Wide Support" (1942) — 202
    Document 4: H.R. 2447, An Act to Grant the Congressional Gold Medal to the Montford Point Marines (2011) — 202

PART VII
QUESTIONS TO CONSIDER — 207
    Constructing a Usable Narrative — 209
    Examining Multiple Interpretations — 210
    Critically Investigating the Research Methodology — 212
    Engaging with the Original Video Footage — 213
    Reflecting — 213

Glossary — 215

LIST OF MAPS

Training camps of the US Marine Corps in 1942 *23*

Train journeys to Montford Point taken by the veterans whose stories are featured in *The First Black Marines* *24*

Locations in the Pacific where Montford Pointers served in World War II *102-103*

PREFACE

This is a book about the first African American Marines, who joined a previously racially exclusive service between 1942 and 1949 and who endured a segregated training program. As much as possible, it follows an approach of honoring and authentically presenting the stories of these men, both collectively and through the oral histories of six individuals who were among the last surviving members of this group. The four authors of the book, scholars and activists of varying backgrounds and skillsets, have done our best to present histories in which these men and their families and communities would recognize themselves. We also seek to accurately represent the messages they wish to leave to future generations.

This book was truly the work of a community. The authors would like to thank many who contributed. These include the veterans themselves, and also the next generations of the National Montford Point Marine Association, family members, and friends who honor and assist them. Of particular assistance in this project were Major Brenda Threatt, Sergeant Major Charles Cook, NMPMA Presidents Dr. James Averhart and Carmen E. Cole (deceased), Monique Braxton, Brenda McDowell, Eric Wilcots, David Wilcots, Willis Gray, and Odell Young.

We are also deeply thankful for the collaboration of an expert film crew led by US Navy veteran and Professor of Cinema Daniel Bernardi and MFA student Jesse Sutterly. We deeply appreciate a generous donation from the Boeing Corporation for the support of this project, as well as donations from friends and family of the authors. Among the moral and financial contributors were Jennifer and Wayne Getz, Jessica Getz, Stacey and Robert Kertsman, William Reginald Grant, Neville Richardson, and the fearsome foursome—Monique, Gillian, Sydney, and Binker.

Our formal and informal editors were also invaluable, especially Rachel Moore, and Charles Cavaliere and Carolin Cichy at Oxford University Press.

We are grateful for the many good suggestions offered by reviewers of our proposal, as well as the close reading of the manuscript provided by several outside readers, including Jacynda Ammons (Missouri State

University), Margaret B. Bodemer (California Polytechnic State University, San Luis Obispo), Reginald K. Ellis (Florida A&M University), Willie Griffin (University of North Carolina at Charlotte), Kenneth Heineman (Angelo State University), Nicholas Juravich (University of Massachusetts Boston), Jennifer Lawrence (Tarrant County College), Mary Lyons-Carmona (University of Nebraska Omaha), J. Todd Moye (University of North Texas), Toni Nicholas (Red Rocks Community College), Brian Peterson (Shasta College), Christian Pinnen (Mississippi College), Tara Ross (Onondaga Community College), Michael Smith (Ithaca College), Suzanne E. Smith (George Mason University), Linda Tomlinson (Fayetteville State University), William Wantland (Mount Vernon Nazarene University), and Melissa Ziobro (Monmouth University). We hope you are pleased with *The First Black Marines* as much as we are.

This book also serves in part as a contribution to the endless struggle to develop a better method for conducting accurate and authentic oral history projects. As such, we particularly owe thanks to scholars like Nepia Mahuika, who have been our methodological and ethical guides.

The photographs in this book have been collected by one of the coauthors, Master Gunnery Sergeant Joseph H. Geeter III, over many years. They are shared in this book courtesy of the National Montford Point Marine Association.

Finally, where would this book be without the veterans? First Sergeant William "Jack" McDowell was the visionary who made this all possible. His story is entangled with that of Staff Sergeant Dave Culmer, Sergeant Henry Wilcots, Sergeant Henry Johnson, Gunnery Sergeant Roosevelt Farrow, and Master Gunnery Sergeant Carroll Braxton. We thank them for their generosity of mind and spirit and their service, both as Marines and as parents, mentors, educators, and workers.

During the writing of this book, one of our participants, Sergeant Henry Johnson, passed away. We mourn the loss of this wonderful man, a beautiful singer and a veteran who served our country. We were privileged to have been able to meet him. He, and the other veterans interviewed in this book, are a small proportion of the approximately 20,000 Marines who passed through Montford Point. We honor these pioneers, as we honor earlier pioneers, including Crispus Attucks (1723–1770).

ABOUT THE AUTHORS AND THE ILLUSTRATOR

Trevor R. Getz is Professor of African and World History at San Francisco State University. His first graphic history, *Abina and the Important Men*, won the 2014 James Harvey Robinson Prize, and he is the recipient of the American Historical Association's 2020 Eugene Asher Distinguished Teaching Award. He is a historian consultant for Veteran Documentary Corps and has written, associate-produced, or produced fourteen profiles of veterans for the Veteran Administration's *Veteran Legacy Program*.

Master Gunnery Sergeant Joseph H. Geeter III, USMC retired, enlisted in the Marine Corps in 1976 and spent twenty-five years on active duty. He served as the 16th President of the National Montford Point Marine Association, Inc., and was instrumental in successfully lobbying the US Congress for the Congressional Gold Medal for these pioneering Marines. He currently commands the Philadelphia Chapter #1 of the organization.

Robert Willis is a public historian. A student of cinema and history, he is driven by a desire to construct effective ways to communicate to the masses and to enrich the lives of people who look like him.

Liz Clarke is a professional illustrator based in Cape Town, South Africa. She has contributed to a variety of graphic history publications, including several titles in the Graphic History Series published by Oxford University Press.

PART I
THE GRAPHIC HISTORY

CHAPTER 1
WHEN I GROW UP

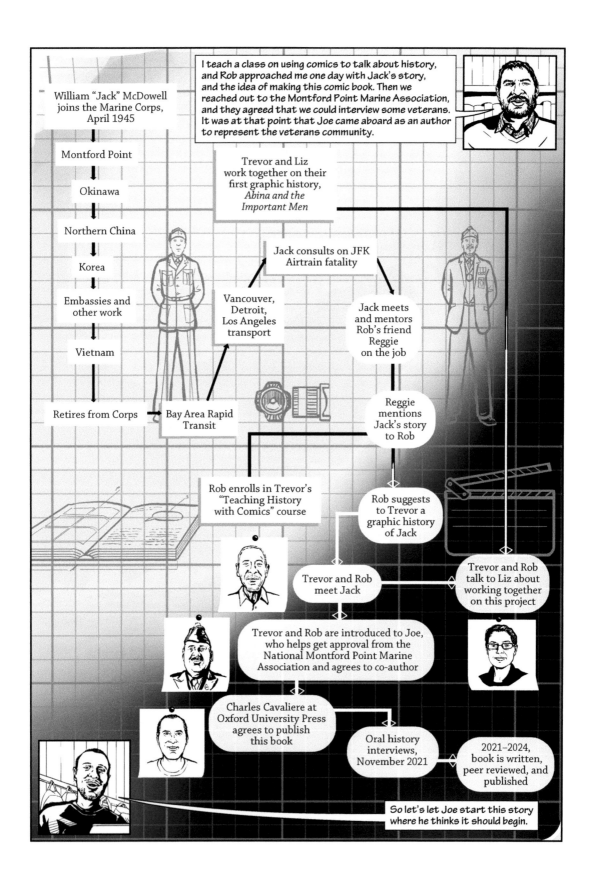

African Americans began to serve even before we were a country. On the 5th of March, 1770, while still British subjects, Americans stood up for their rights. They were against all the taxes that King George was imposing and they rebelled in Boston. And some of the British troops shot and killed some Americans. And the first one to fall was a gentleman named Crispus Attucks. And he was an African American, a sailor, and a free man.

William L. Champney. (fl. 1850-1857). Boston Massacre, March 5th, 1770. Boston, Published by Henry Q. Smith. Chromolithograph.

The National Archives https://catalog.archives.gov/id/518262

And it is hereby ordered as follows:

1. All departments and agencies of the Government of the United States concerned with vocational and training programs for defense production shall take special measures appropriate to assure that such programs are administered without discrimination because of race, creed, color, or national origin;

2. All contracting agencies of the Government of the United States shall include in all defense contracts hereafter negotiated by them a provision obligating the contractor not to discriminate against any worker because of race, creed, color, or national origin ...

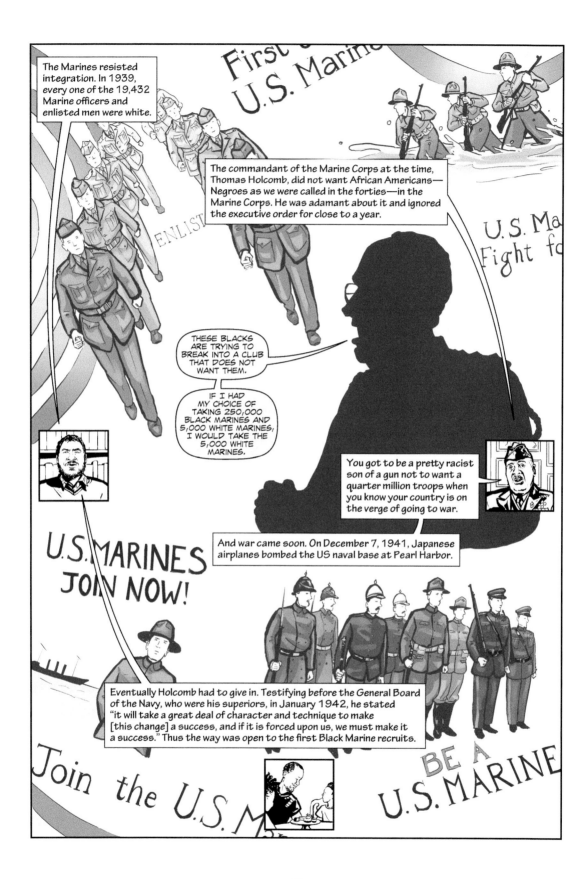

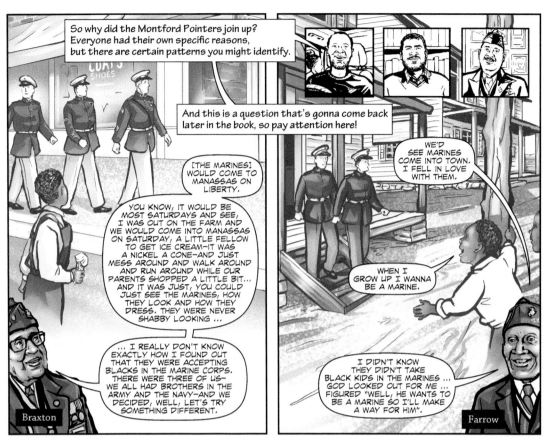

CHAPTER 2
WHERE HELL STARTS

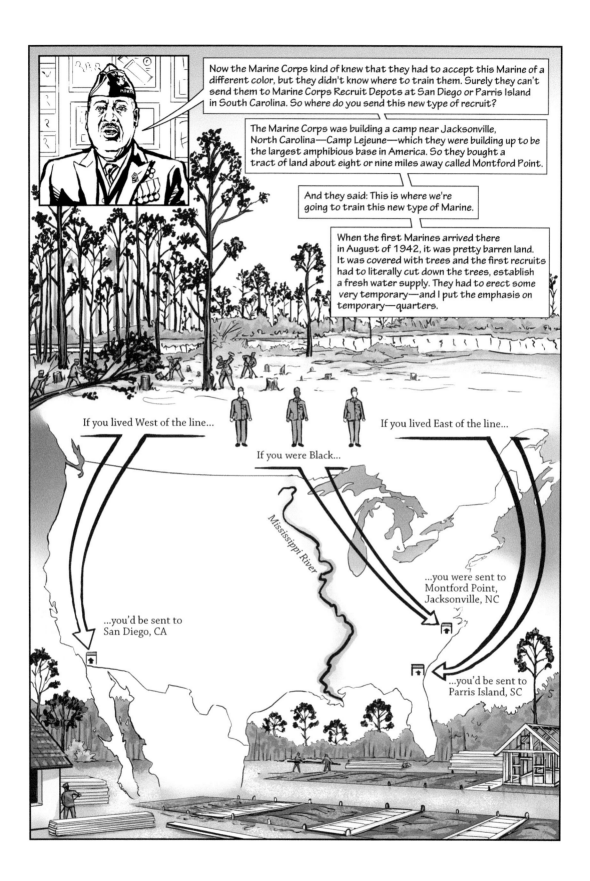

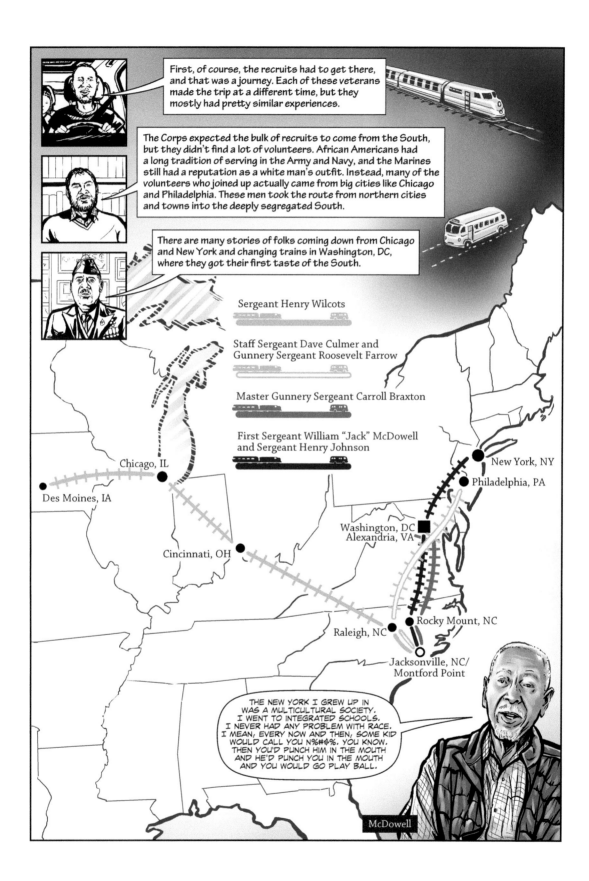

CHAPTER 3
BLACK MARINES IN JIM CROW AMERICA

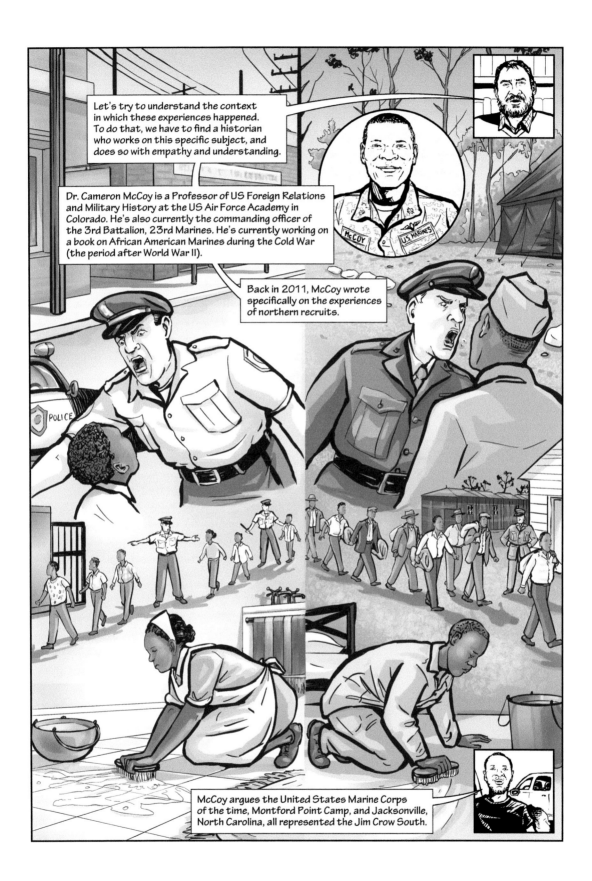

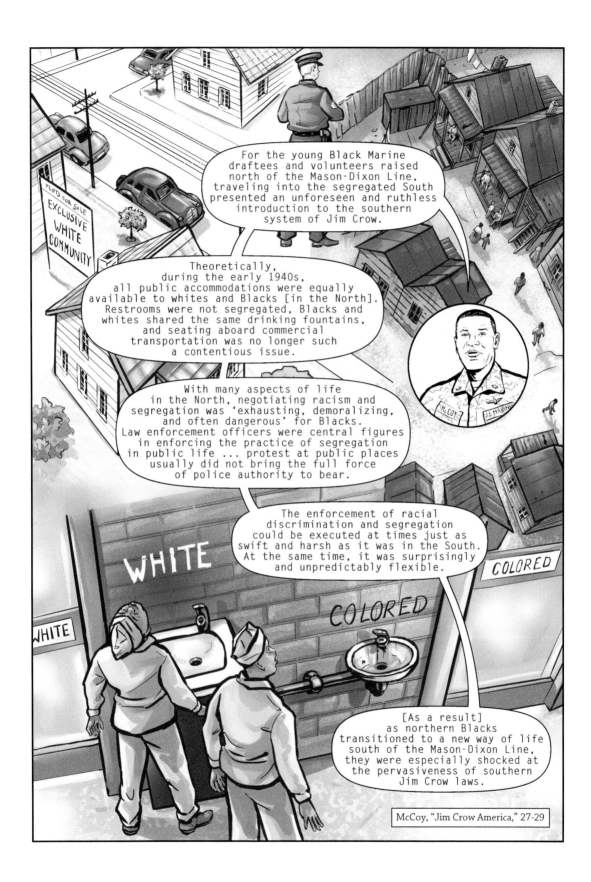

This pattern matches the wider experience of hundreds of thousands of Black Americans who served in other branches of the US military during World War II, most of whom went through training camps in the US South. Historian Charles Postel studies evidence from these sailors and GIs, including letters they sent home. Here are some of those letters he shared with me:

Mother, you want to know the truth about it down here, well to make it short, 'It's Hell.' They treat you so rotten down here, you sometimes wonder if you're a human being ... Sometimes I wonder if I'll leave here in one piece.

— Letter from Daniel Reeves to his mother, Camp Van Dorn, Mississippi, 1943

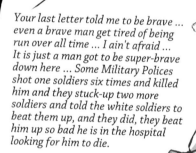

Your last letter told me to be brave ... even a brave man get tired of being run over all time ... I ain't afraid ... It is just a man got to be super-brave down here ... Some Military Polices shot one soldiers six times and killed him and they stuck-up two more soldiers and told the white soldiers to beat them up, and they did, they beat him up so bad he is in the hospital looking for him to die.

— Jack Walker to his mother, Fort Benning, Georgia, 1941

When I first arrived, our sector actually looked like a garbage dump in comparison with the rest of the camp is completely ostracized from the camp proper so we rarely see the other group. Our living quarters are terrible being ... located just in from the camp cesspool.

— Bert B. Babero to Truman K. Gibson, Camp Barkeley, Texas, 1944

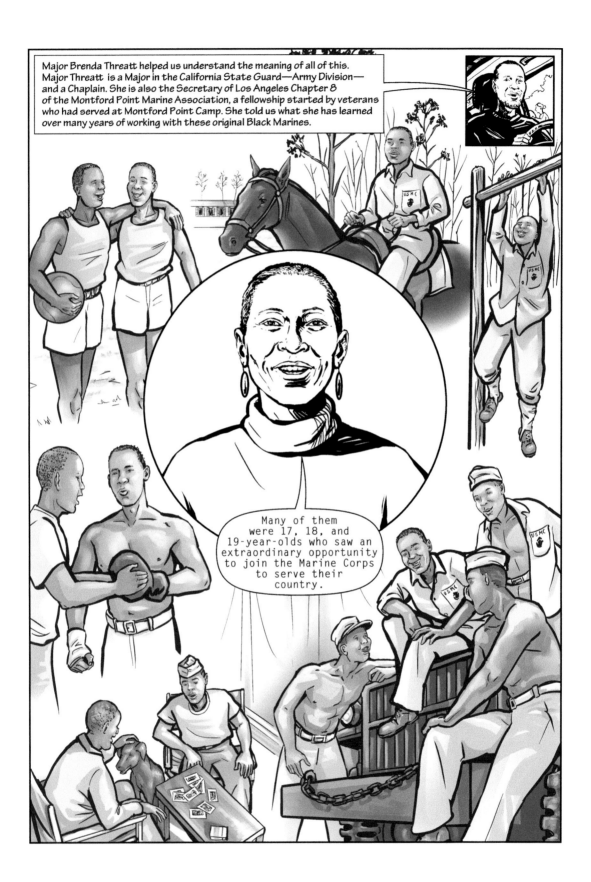

CHAPTER 4
LET THE MOSQUITOES EAT

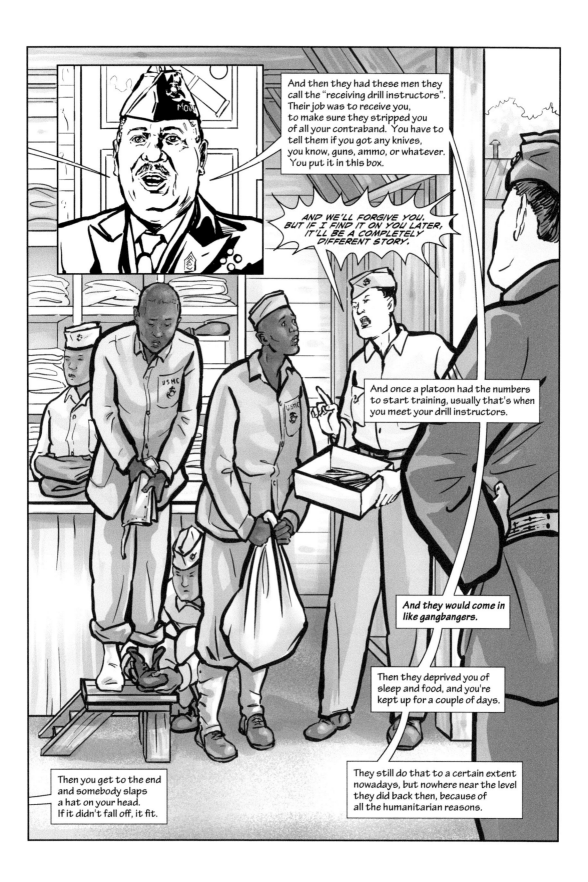

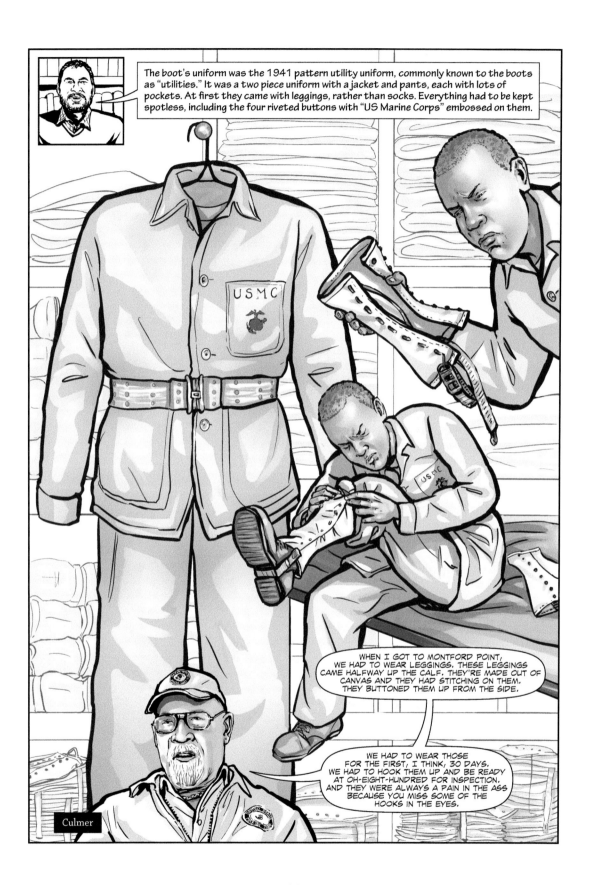

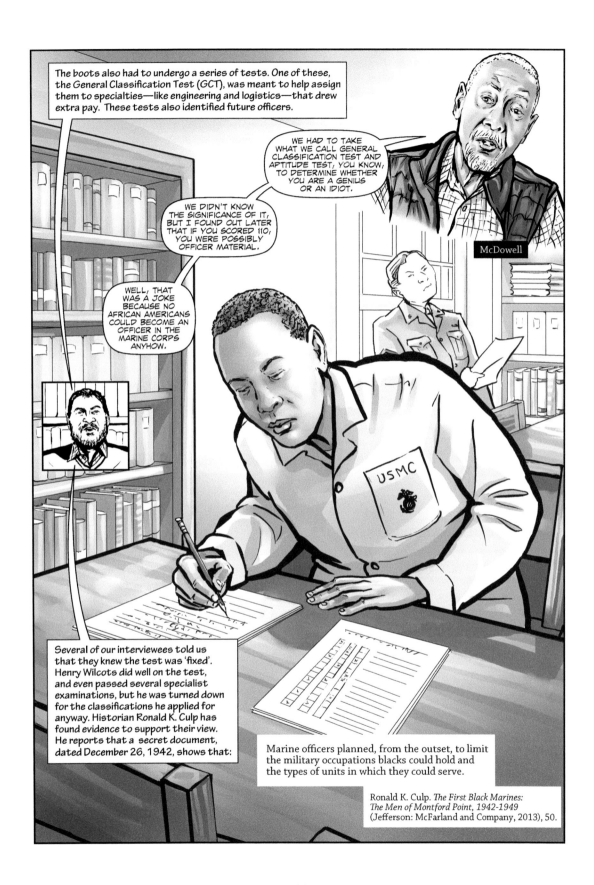

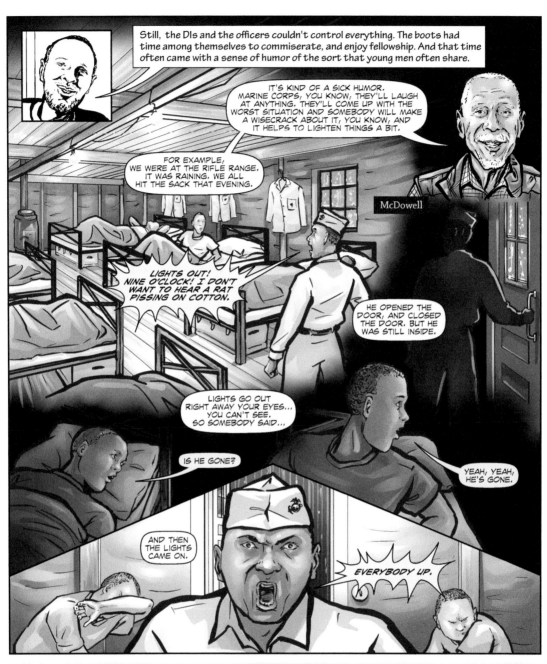

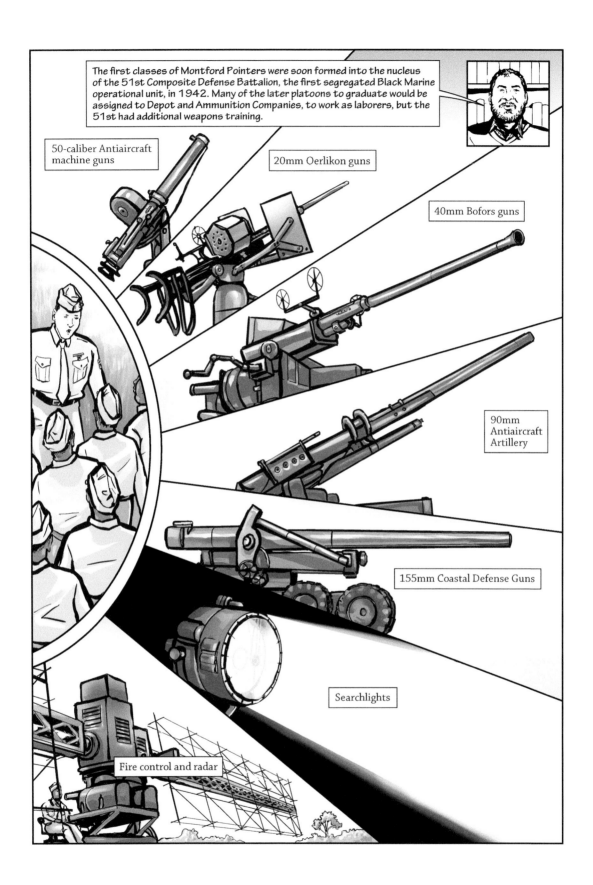

CHAPTER 5
ALL OF THEM ARE LEGENDARY

Then an opportunity came up in the spring of 1943—just about seven months after Montford Point was established—and it was decided that Blacks would now be trained as drill instructors. Well, they pretty much knew who they wanted to have.

And they did some good picking.

I mean if you look at those first six drill instructors, all of them are legendary. Two especially.

There was Sergeant Major Huff—PFC Huff at the time—the first African American Sergeant Major promoted from the ranks of Marine Corps, the first to serve 30 years. He was just revered throughout the Marine Corps, by everyone, Black and white.

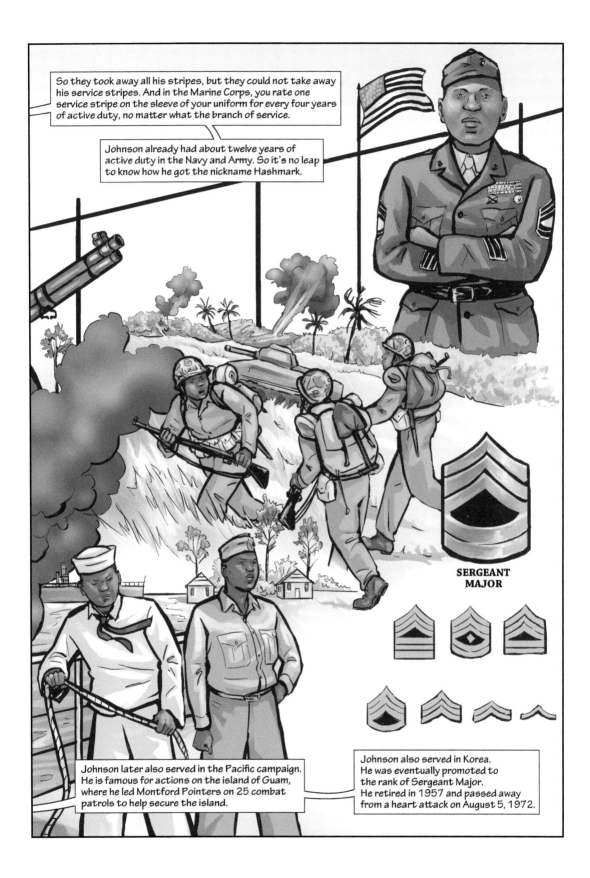

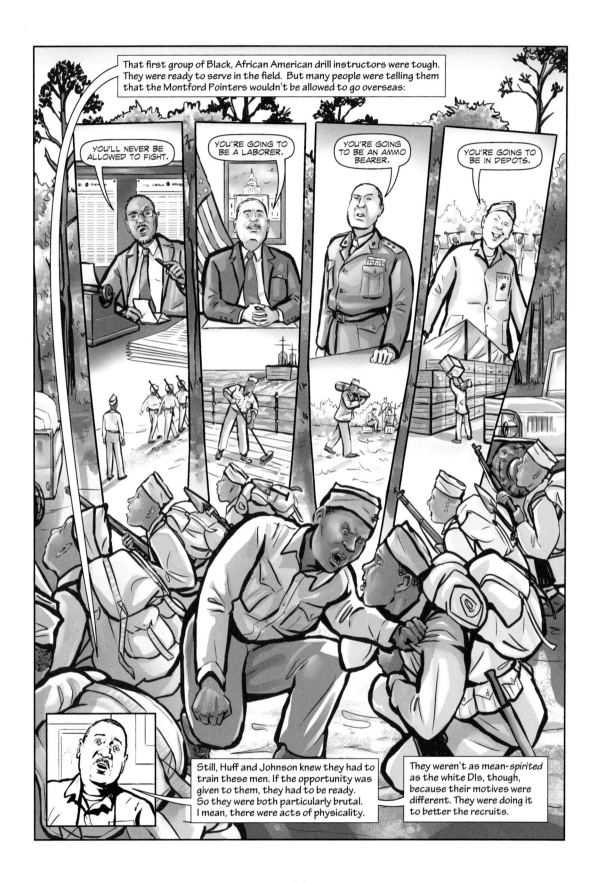

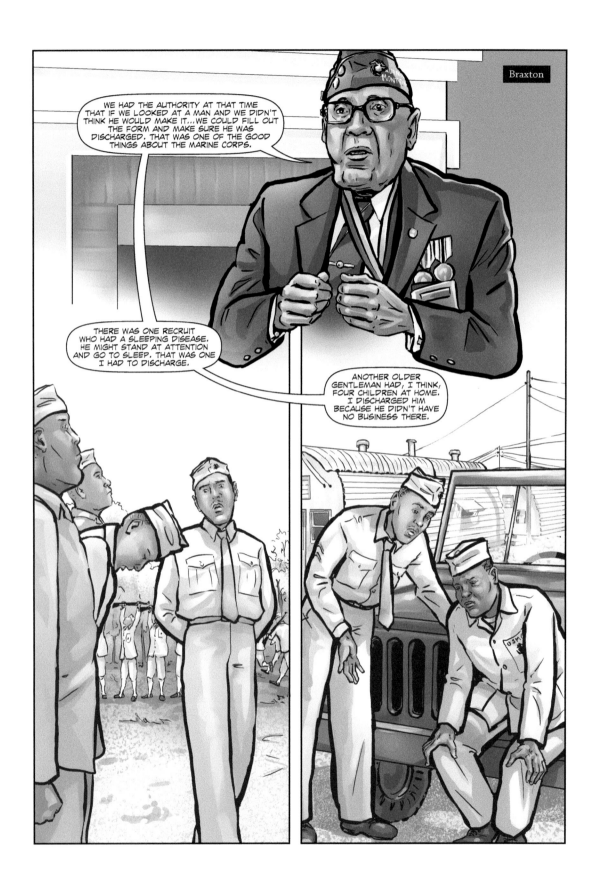

CHAPTER 6
A 17-YEAR-OLD KID WITH A .45 PISTOL

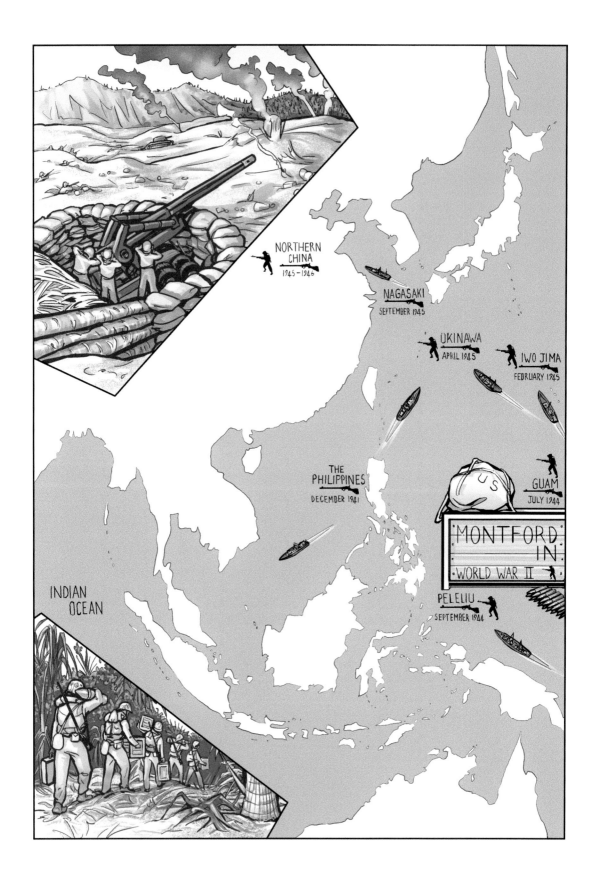

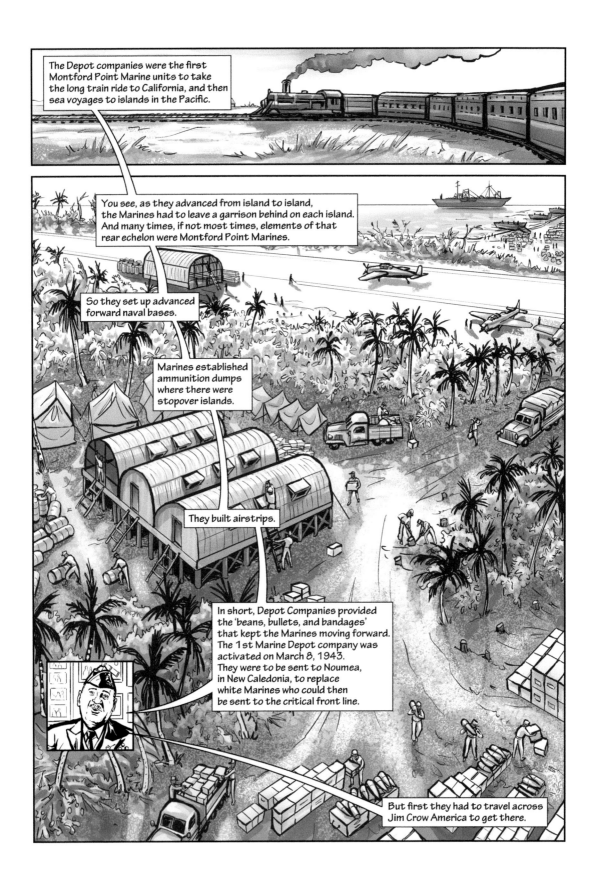

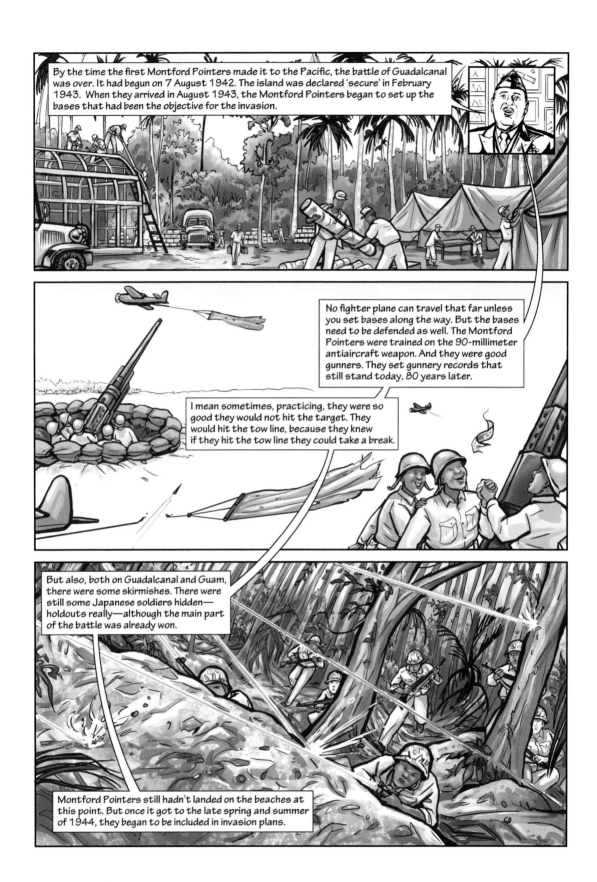

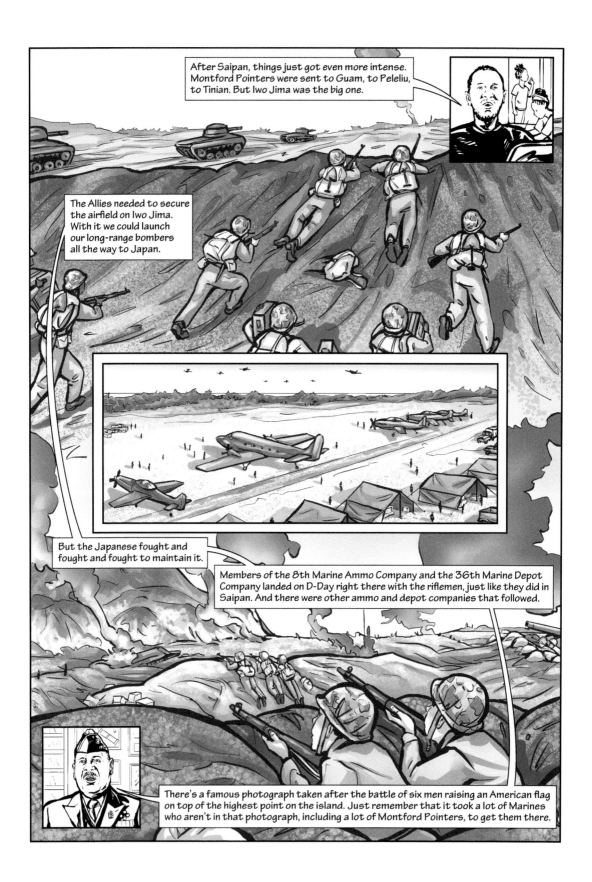

CHAPTER 7
AFTERMATHS AND LEGACIES

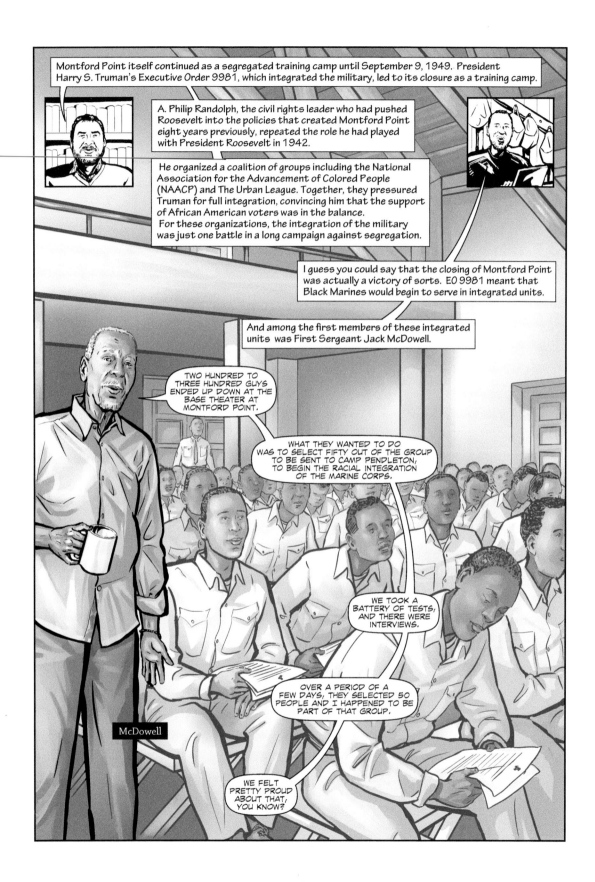

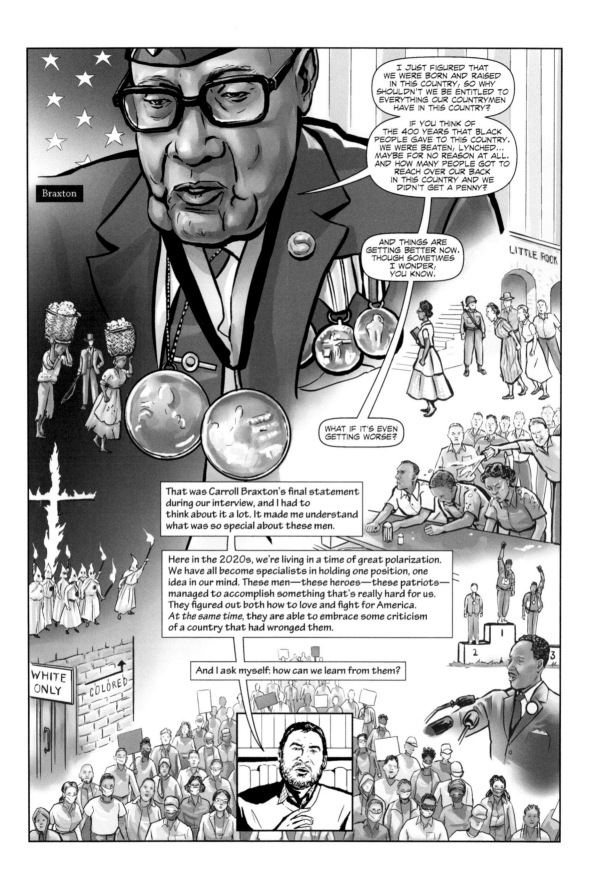

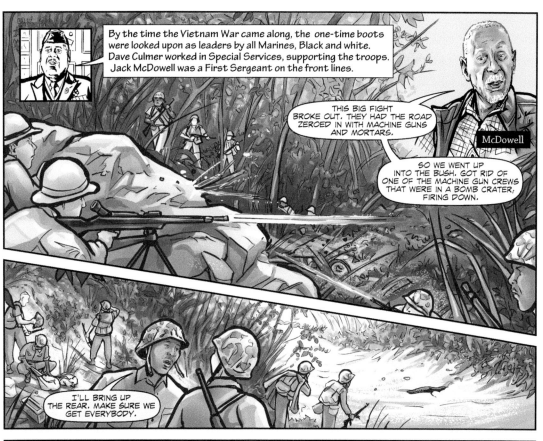

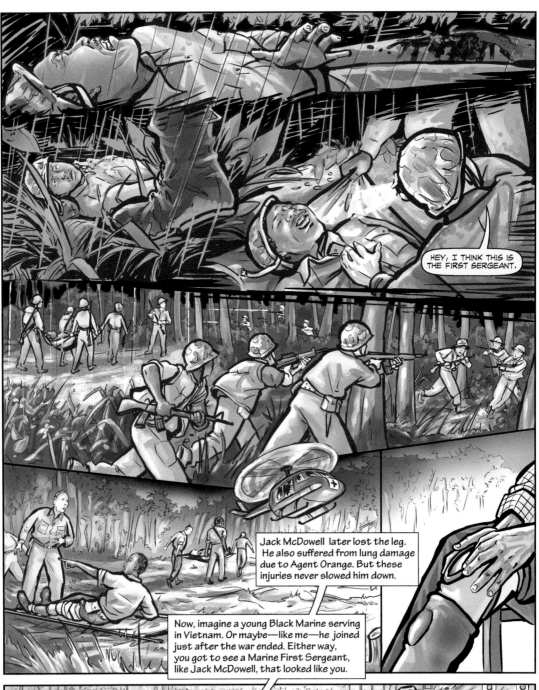

PART II
STARTING A RESEARCH PROJECT

INTRODUCTION

This book is the result of a research project that brought together a group of people with very different skills who wanted to know more about the world they lived in and how it came to be. One by one, they slowly became interested in understanding—and helping others to understand—the individual and collective stories of a group of African American veterans who had joined the US Marine Corps between 1942 and 1949. In the order by which we became involved, this group includes Master Gunnery Sergeant Joseph H. Geeter III, public historian Robert Willis, academic historian Trevor R. Getz, artist Liz Clarke, and editors Charles Cavaliere and Carolin Cichy.

Of course, this book is not about this group of historians, artists, and editors. Rather, it is primarily the story of six of the first Black US Marines, or Montford Point Marines. They are First Sergeant William "Jack" McDowell, Sergeant Henry Wilcots, Staff Sergeant Dave Culmer, Master Gunnery Sergeant Carroll Braxton, Gunnery Sergeant Roosevelt Farrow, and Sergeant Henry Johnson, all retired. They are all men, a subject we will discuss later. Their titles are the ranks at which they retired, but they all began their time in the Corps as **boots**—young recruits at Montford Point Camp, a segregated Marine Corps training facility that operated during and immediately after the Second World War.

This book came about because Willis and Getz wanted to learn more about these first Black Marines, and later approached the other authors to help them in their endeavor. To answer our questions, we designed and carried out a historical research project using what is known as the **inquiry model**. This is a general model that is adaptable for research at every level—from a classroom project to the largest professional scholarly pursuit. We used this model to progress from questions to answers in our research project—and then presented those answers in the form of a graphic **interpretation**. In this section, we describe our inquiry model approach. We do this for three reasons:

- First, we want to demonstrate this general method of doing historical research and interpretation.
- Second, we want to provide you with an account of our work so that you can use it to critically assess our approach and findings for yourself.

- Finally, we want to highlight some important features of undertaking this kind of work, in particular ways of working with a community and doing oral history work effectively and ethically.

In the sections that follow, you will be able to follow along with us as we go through important stages of an inquiry approach to research. Broadly, these stages are:

- Define the questions to which you are seeking answers.
- Read the material others have already produced on this topic, which may help you to answer your questions.
- Explore the historical context and environment in which the people you are studying lived and acted.
- Do the research to find answers to the questions you have asked. In the case of the Montford Point Marines, this was mostly through the oral history method.
- Interpret the material you gather through your research in order to determine answers to the questions you have asked.
- Finally, communicate what you have learned to others.

DEFINING QUESTIONS

Like many great stories, this project started with the "discovery" of a single source that the researchers found fascinating and wanted to know more about. In this case, the source wasn't a document, but rather a human being. As we diagram on page 10, the origins of this project begin with Jack McDowell, an African American veteran, telling his story to a colleague, who then shared it with the first of our authors—Rob Willis. This encounter started a sequence of events and conversations about Jack's experiences and those of his fellow Montford Pointers. Of the three historians who eventually collaborated on the project, Joe Geeter already knew a lot about these veterans, but Rob and his fellow historian Trevor Getz did not. So they formulated some questions to which they wanted answers. These became the research questions that guided our inquiry as a team:

- What were the experiences of the Montford Point Marines?
- What do these experiences tell us about the military and American society during the Second World War?
- What is the legacy of the Montford Point Marines, and what messages do they want to share with our society today?

At the time, these three questions seemed useful for a variety of reasons. Like most good research questions, each of them focused on a topic that was specific enough to make it possible to find thorough answers to them. Additionally, those answers could be determined through research, especially research using the methodology of **oral history**. Finally, all three were significant questions. In other words, we felt that they would yield answers that would be meaningful to us and to the audience we wanted to reach.

Equally importantly, these questions gave us a lot of different angles through which to cover the history of the Montford Point Marines. While the first question is primarily focused on facts, the other two are more concerned with perspectives and messages. Also, two questions are specific to the Montford Pointers, while the third one connects them to their society and historical context. One is about the legacy of the Montford Pointers and their messages *today*, but the other two cover the events and experiences of the past.

Are these the *right* questions to ask about the Montford Point Marines? There are many different questions that one might ask about this significant group of men and the communities and societies with which they have interacted—and other questions may have led us to answers that would have shed light on this history from a different angle. But these three questions are the ones that gave us a clearly defined place to start looking for answers and set in motion the inquiry process that would lead to this book.

BUILDING A CRITICAL BIBLIOGRAPHY

Once we had a set of questions, we set out to learn everything we could about the Montford Point Marines. Setting up interviews with the surviving veterans was going to take a while, and we used the intervening time to find out what previous scholars had written. We were not the first researchers to write about the Montford Point Marines—although we may be the first team to include a Marine, a public historian, and an artist along with a formally trained historian! By the time we started our project, other historians had already completed much valuable work to uncover the history of both the camp and the men who passed through it.

Our approach to reviewing the existing literature on the Montford Point Marines was to construct a **critical bibliography**. A critical bibliography is a description and evaluation of all of the scholarly work a researcher can find on a topic. It allows us to explore and understand the work that other scholars have already done on this subject. Understanding this previous work helps researchers to shape their own research. Sometimes we find ways to build on and extend the existing understanding of the topic. Often we merely identify a perspective or approach that is missing and try to rectify that absence. And at yet other times, we find that we disagree with what has been written before we started our own investigations, and need to challenge it with a new interpretation. In any case, it is important to understand that it is just about impossible to contribute to and grow our knowledge about a topic unless we are aware of what work has already been done.

For this project, three particular sets of written histories shaped the questions we asked and the meaning we took away from the interviews we conducted with members of the Montford Point Marines. You will find that we reference these books and articles throughout the sections that follow, and some of these scholars are highlighted in the graphic narrative, especially where their theories were particularly significant. We also want to collect them together in this one section so that we can describe to you how each one was useful to us and how our work differs from them. These three sets of writing are:

- Histories of African Americans in the military, which helped us to understand the continuities and changes experienced by Black servicemembers over time and especially during the Second World War.
- Histories of the Montford Point Marines specifically, both to provide valuable context for understanding the oral histories we collected and to introduce key themes and issues in the history of this group of servicemembers.
- Biographies and autobiographies of Montford Pointers, mostly written or spoken by veterans themselves and therefore helping us identify themes in the experiences and perspectives of the Montford Pointers.

This is not an exhaustive list of all of the books or articles on these topics. Rather, it is an account we created of the most important works we read to prepare for this project, and those we returned to often as we wrote this book.

AFRICAN AMERICANS IN THE MILITARY

African Americans have a long and storied history of service in the United States military. In the graphic narrative portion of this book, Joe Geeter recounts some of this history, and you can find out more about it from a number of insightful works on the topic, including two written by veterans. The first of these is Bernard Nalty's *Strength for the Fight*, which was first published in the mid-1980s. Nalty, who also wrote a short work on African American Marines that we will turn to later, was an officer in the US Army, a civilian historian for the US Marine Corps, and later also worked for the Office of Air Force History. His book provides a framework of facts and events for understanding the experience of Black soldiers, sailors, airmen, and Marines.[1] Gerald Astor, a journalist and Second World War infantryman, followed this book up in 2001 with *The Right to Fight*, a much more narrative and experience-focused account of African Americans in the military across US History.[2]

Despite books such as these, the full extent of the service and contributions of African Americans during the Second World War in particular is still often hidden from broader American audiences. Although many African American families know about their grandparents' or parents' service, Black Americans have not tended to appear much in Hollywood movies about World War II or best-selling popular history books on the topic. Still, important work has been done and can be found, if you look for it. One very important book from the 1980s is *Taps for a Jim Crow Army*, a collection of letters from Black soldiers in training camps and overseas, written to parents, advocacy organizations, superior officers, and the government. These letters, collected and edited by historian Phillip McGuire, remain an important tool for understanding the experiences—and witnessing the resistance and organizing—of Black soldiers during the war.[3]

Between 2000 and 2012, films like *Red Tails*, *Hart's War*, and *Miracle at St. Anna* helped counteract American ignorance about the contributions of Black Americans to the Second World War. At the same time, several scholarly histories that also contributed to raising awareness for the important role that Black soldiers played in the war appeared. Two particularly important volumes bookend these years. The first of these was Maggi Morehouse's *Fighting in the Jim Crow Army*, a book that emerged from accounts she found of her father's service as a white officer in the almost all-Black 93rd Infantry Division. Morehouse interviewed fifty veterans of the unit and built her book around their accounts.[4] The second is *The Fog of War*, which came out in 2012—the same year as the movie *Red Tails*. This collection of essays describes the relationships between African American service in the war and the development of the **civil rights movement**. Although its organization into separate essays by different authors means that it is more of a series of deep dives rather than a broad and comprehensive survey of the topic, it brought together the important

---

1 Bernard C. Nalty, *Strength for the Fight: A History of Black Americans in the Military* (Free Press, 1986).
2 Gerald Astor, *The Right to Fight: A History of African Americans in the Military* (Da Capo Press, 2001).
3 Phillip McGuire, editor, *Taps for a Jim Crow Army: Letters from Black Soldiers in World War II* (University Press of Kentucky, 1983).
4 Maggi M. Morehouse, *Fighting in the Jim Crow Army: Black Men and Women Remember World War II* (Rowman & Littlefield, 2000).

work of many scholars.[5] Their essays helped us to understand some of the accounts of Montford Pointers about the 1950s in particular. They also contextualized the often complex responses the veterans we interviewed gave when we asked them questions about their experiences with race and racism during the Second World War.

Two very recent histories have brought this body of research up to date: Matthew F. Delmont's *Half American*[6] and Thomas A. Guglielmo's *Divisions*.[7] Both books demonstrate the ways in which American racism held back the country's war effort, but whereas Delmont's work focuses entirely on Black Americans, Guglielmo weaves together the experiences of Japanese Americans and African Americans. Both scholars arrive at similar assessments of the continuities and changes of the war era. Delmont argues that although the United States could not have achieved victory against Nazi Germany and Imperial Japan without the contributions of African Americans, it was unable to vanquish white supremacy at home. In chapter after chapter, he shows that many white Americans were willing to impede the war effort in order to maintain their racial privileges. In similar fashion, Guglielmo focuses on unraveling the myth that, through the war, Americans learned to unite for the common good. Instead, he reveals the divisions that continued to shape the lives, experiences, and deaths of minoritized Americans through and after the war. Both books are a response to the common American memory of the "good war" and the "greatest generation"—the two frames through which most Americans make sense of the Second World War. The "good war" frame situates the United States as part of a purely "good" coalition justly fighting "evil" enemies. The "greatest generation" frame venerates Americans who were adults during World War II for their sacrifices and perseverance. Neither frame is without merit, but they tend to make it hard to talk about issues like race, segregation, and discrimination during the war years.

Taken together, these two books provide context and a framework for interpreting the experiences of the veterans featured in this book. However, they are more critical of the American war effort than most of the veterans we interviewed. When the time arrived for us to interpret the experiences of those veterans, we found that we sometimes had to depart from these accounts in order to authentically represent what the veterans told us.

---

5 Kevin M. Kruse and Stephen Tuck, *Fog of War: The Second World War and the Civil Rights Movement* (Oxford University Press, 2012).
6 Matthew F. Delmont, *Half American: The Epic Story of African Americans Fighting World War II at Home and Abroad* (Viking, 2022).
7 Thomas A. Guglielmo, *Divisions: A New History of Racism and Resistance in America's World War II Military* (Oxford University Press, 2021).

One important history of African Americans in World War II that shaped our writing has not yet been published. We would like to thank historian Charles Postel for allowing us to read draft chapters from a forthcoming history that was started by the legendary researcher and teacher Leon Litwack, and which Postel is completing. The chapters we read focused in particular on the experiences of Black servicemen and women, and are the result of decades of work.[8]

There are not many books that deal specifically with the experience of African American servicemen in the Pacific—the war against Japan. You may wonder if a book dealing only with this theater of operations might be necessary. After all, were not all Black men in the US military at the time dealing with the same general racial context, regardless of where they served? Chris Dixon suggests that there may have been some unique factors in the Pacific that make it worth examining separately in his book *African Americans and the Pacific War 1941–1945*.[9] Dixon points out that the War in the Pacific largely took place in former European colonies which had their own subjugated populations and racial order, which created unique contexts for the African Americans who were based on these islands. Also, the war was fought against the Japanese, who often represented themselves as the liberators of people oppressed by white populations. The Japanese, therefore, aimed their propaganda not only at the populations of the islands they captured but also, to some degree, at African Americans. Finally, through these campaigns, Black sailors and soldiers came into contact with majority white populations that did not have social systems as oppressive as America's Jim Crow, especially in Australia. For Dixon, this story also has deep gender elements in the way that US military officers understood the masculinity of African American men. Dominant strands of American society at the time saw Black servicemen as a danger to women. In the context of the war in the Pacific, this perception was worsened by the widespread racialized conception of Polynesian and Asian women as submissive and compliant. The result was policies that restricted Black servicemen's movements and liberties in populated areas while allowing white servicemen access to local women. These elements provide important contextual information and insights that we need to bear in mind throughout our efforts to understand what the experience of the Montford Point Marines was like once they left the United States and served in Guam, Saipan, Okinawa, Peleliu, Iwo Jima, and eventually Japan itself.

---

8 Leon F. Litwack and Charles Postel, *Pearl Harbor Blues: Black Americans in the World War II Era* (forthcoming).
9 Chris Dixon, *African Americans and the Pacific War 1941–1945: Race, Nationality, and the Fight for Freedom* (Cambridge University Press, 2018).

MONTFORD POINT MARINES

What scholarly works are available that focus specifically on the African American men who joined the United States Marine Corps and trained at Montford Point Camp from its inception in 1942 until it was closed in 1949?

Several official texts have been commissioned to memorialize the history of African Americans in the Marine Corp. The first one is Henry I. Shaw Jr. and Ralph W. Donnelly's *Blacks in the Marine Corps*, which was published in 1975 and laid the foundation for all research on the Montford Point Marines that has followed since.[10] This book began with Donnelly's painstaking research into thousands of files in official military archives, supplemented by interviews Shaw conducted with significant Black officers as well as Black enlisted men and veterans. The book focuses mainly on the World War II era but extends through the Korean Conflict into the Vietnam War, a conflict that was just coming to an end when the book was published, and where—the authors note—questions of racism in the Corps had come into focus once again. Although less focused on individual perspectives or collective experiences than we might be today, this work provided a pathway and a framework for understanding the stories of Montford Pointers.

The second official publication was *Right to Fight: African American Marines in World War II*. Its author, Bernard C. Nalty, was a civilian member of the Marine Corps history program when he wrote this book—which could also be considered an extended pamphlet—in 1994.[11] Developed to commemorate the 50th anniversary of the Second World War, the result is a fact-filled chronology of the Montford Pointers. While not shying away from the discrimination faced by these Marines, Nalty focuses on sketching a structure of major decisions and events rather than delving deep into human experiences or producing new interpretations. The book does highlight a number of important figures and events that have become central to the myth and history of Montford Pointers: the much-appreciated Colonel Samuel L. Woods, the two legendary drill instructors Edgar R. Huff and Gilbert H. "Hashmark" Johnson, and the so-called Death Route protests at Montford Point Camp. As a semi-official publication, the book is generally favorable to the Corps. It ends on a positive note suggesting that the Marines had fully committed to racial integration by the late 1960s. As some of the oral histories that we collected reveal, this was not entirely the case.

---

10 Henry I. Shaw Jr. and Ralph W. Donnelly, *Blacks in the Marine Corps* (History and Museums Division, Headquarters, US Marine Corps, 1975; reprint 2002).
11 Bernard C. Nalty, *The Right to Fight: African-American Marines in World War II* (History and Museums Division, Headquarters, US Marine Corps, 1994).

Beyond these semi-official texts, the two best-known published histories of the Montford Point Marines are Melton McLaurin's *Marines of Montford Point* and Ronald Culp's *First Black United States Marines*.[12] These are two quite different books. McLaurin's slim volume is composed of excerpts from interviews with sixty-one veterans that cover anything from their decision to join the Corps through to their experience of combat, with an extensive section focused on Montford Point camp itself. Culp's work, by contrast, is a chronological history of the formation, training, and service of African American Marines based largely on documentary sources produced by the clerks and officers of the Corps. The two volumes complement each other, however, and present a single coherent narrative. They tell the story of both reluctant and enthusiastic recruits arriving at a newly purposed but run-down camp in the Jim Crow South—recruits who were anxious to prove themselves as equal to white Marines but faced significant obstacles along the way. When they headed into the Pacific, they were meant to serve as labor and defense units only, but eventually had to join combat. Culp's text is valuable in providing a detailed scaffold of facts, events, campaigns, and policy changes over time. The carefully curated account in McLaurin's volume adds the individual human stories to flesh out this framework. Together, they form the kind of groundwork that researchers like us needed to understand the experiences and perspectives of the Montford Point Marines.

The next works on the Montford Pointers as a whole that were vital to our project were written by Cameron McCoy, himself an African American Marine as well as a historian. McCoy's work mostly takes the form of two unpublished works. The first is his master's thesis in history completed at Texas A&M University, "Jim Crow America and the Marines of Montford Point in the World War II Era."[13] This work was most importantly an interpretation of the experiences that a small number of Black Marines from the northern states lived through in the Jim Crow South. As a successor to these men himself, McCoy particularly wanted to know why they had chosen to join a branch of the military that had denied them membership until forced to change.

McCoy's next work was his PhD dissertation at the University of Texas.[14] This work also reflected McCoy's own experiences and status,

---

12 Melton A. McLaurin, *Marines of Montford Point: America's First Black Marines* (University of North Carolina Press, 2007); Ronald K. Culp, *First Black United States Marines: The Men of Montford Point, 1942–1946* (McFarland & Company, 2007).
13 Cameron Demetrius McCoy, "Jim Crow America and the Marines of Montford Point in the World War II Era" (MA thesis, Texas A&M University, 2011).
14 Cameron Demetrius McCoy, "Mr. President, What of the Marines? The Politic of Contested Integration and the Domestic Legacy of the Modern Black Letherneck in Cold War America" (PhD diss., University of Texas Austin, 2017).

and mostly focused on the long legacy of the Montford Pointers and the slow rate of change in the Corps. It particularly considered the long delays in full integration and the promotion of Black officers in the Marine Corps, which happened as late as the Vietnam War. Together, McCoy's two works add both length and depth to the history that McLaurin and Culp had begun to sketch out.[15]

WRITTEN BIOGRAPHY/AUTOBIOGRAPHY

The books and theses described in the previous sections gave us a framework of events and a sense of the collective history of the Montford Pointers and their historical context. But before we started to collect the oral histories of the six Marines featured in this book, we wanted to get a sense of how other Montford Pointers had spoken and written about their experiences. Fortunately, many of these African American veterans left a record of their experiences, often with the help of family members or scholars. In this section, we discuss a few of the autobiographical and biographical works that helped us to formulate our questions and situate the specific oral histories of the Montford Pointers we interviewed in their larger context.

The first biography that deserves special treatment here is Judson Jeffries's fine profile of Colonel Herbert L. Brewer, one of the original Montford Pointers, in the journal *Spectrum*.[16] An intensely thoughtful and respectful biography by an important African American political scientist, this article highlights many of the seeming contradictions within the history of the Montford Pointers. It tells the story of a young man's desire for acceptance into an organization that first rejected him on the basis of race and then denied him easy advancement through the ranks, but eventually provided him with both a home and a career. This ambivalent experience, present in Brewer's story, appears again and again in the stories of the Montford Pointers we interviewed as well.

Montford Pointers have given many interviews and recounted their experiences many times. Some of these accounts can be found in McLaurin's *Marines of Montford Point*, and others can be found on YouTube or in documentary short films. Book-length accounts are more rare, and often get only very limited printings. One very hard to obtain personal account of the Pacific campaign was written by two Montford Point Marine veterans of the 8th Ammunition Company, Perry E. Fisher and Brooks E. Gray.

---

15   The first Black Marines do also appear in one chapter of Morris J. McGregor Jr., *Defense Studies: Integration of the Armed Forces, 1940–1965* (Center of Military History, 1981).
16   Judson L. Jeffries, "Col. Herbert L. Brewer and the United States Marine Corps: A Man of Many Firsts," *Spectrum: A Journal on Black Men* 1 (Autumn 2012): 179–195.

Their *Blacks and Whites Together Through Hell* tells the story of an African American unit that landed alongside white Marines in the bloody invasion of Iwo Jima, and does so from the authors' own first-hand perspectives.[17] *Footprints of the Montford Point Marines* is a particularly innovative book that interweaves a father's first-hand accounts of his service with his son's interpretations of these. This 2022 labor of love is co-credited by author Eugene S. Mosley to his father Thomas Mosley. Through its unusual structure, this book introduces perspectives from two generations, which sets it apart from the other works described here.[18] Another important recent memoir is the self-published *Jack the Marine* by Jack McDowell, which is unfortunately available only to friends and family at this time. But it is still worth mentioning because it helped shape our understanding of this incredible man and Marine.[19]

Together, all of these texts helped the authors build an understanding of the historical context of the memories of the veterans and the stories they told. Without that context, we would have been lost. But it is important to note that we did not see any of these texts as *the* authority. We sought to understand the value of each one, but also its silences and limits. They all told slightly different stories, from different perspectives, and were sometimes challenged or contradicted by each other and by the veterans. Still, we are very aware that we could not have conducted our inquiry without the information and interpretations these authors shared.

---

17 Perry E. Fisher and Brooks E. Gray, *Blacks and Whites Together Through Hell: U.S. Marines in World War II* (Millsmont Publishing, 1993).
18 Eugene S. Mosley and Thomas Mosley, *Footprints of the Montford Point Marines: A Narrative of the Epic Strides in Overcoming the Racial Disparities of the United States Marine Corps* (Dagmar Miura, 2022).
19 William "Jack" McDowell, *Jack the Marine*, self-published, 2023.

PART III
HISTORICAL CONTEXT

You already know that this book is an attempt to understand the memories and messages of a group of individual men. Now, most histories focus on the actions and experiences of a particular group of people. But people don't live in a vacuum. We can't understand the lives and experiences of individuals without at the same time holding in our mind a history of the times and places they lived in. We call this broader history the "historical context."

People's actions, and even their perspectives, are shaped by their environments. That is not to say that individuals do not act to shape their environments in turn. They do! Still, the society in which they live and its institutions can provide opportunities and impose limits on what they can do. For the Montford Point Marines we interviewed for this graphic narrative, there are five main contexts in which we need to understand and situate their experiences: Jim Crow America, the US military, the US Marine Corps and Montford Point Camp in particular, the War in the Pacific, and the experiences of African American veterans at home and in the Corps after the war.

Let's start by looking at the society in which these men grew up.

JIM CROW AMERICA

The Montford Point Marines—African American men who enlisted in the United States Marine Corps and were trained at Montford Point Camp between 1942 and 1949—grew up and came of age in Jim Crow America. Their America was a country that segregated and discriminated against African Americans through law, customs, and practices. This discrimination extended to the Corps, characterized their time at Montford Point, and even followed them overseas into battle.

Now, many of the Montford Pointers we meet today downplay the role that race played in their experiences in one way or another, often suggesting that it was just "silliness" or only one part of their story. Some point out that they grew up in the northern states, where discrimination was less obvious to them, at least until they arrived at Montford Point Camp. Or they want us to know that the Corps eventually grew up, that discrimination lessened in the years following the Second World War, and that the military they served in played a major role in desegregating American society as a whole. Or, as humans are prone to do, they want to smooth over some of their more difficult memories in order to protect themselves.

Still, every one of the men we interviewed recognized that race and racism—in particular the laws, customs, and practices known as **Jim Crow**—have shaped their histories. For approximately two hundred and fifty years, most Black people in North America had been enslaved in horrendous conditions. In February 1865, toward the end of the Civil War, President Abraham Lincoln approved the Joint Resolution of Congress to abolish slavery (though the necessary number of states did not ratify the Thirteenth Amendment until December). In those states that had been in rebellion, Radical Reconstruction promised true political participation and equality for all. The Fourteenth and Fifteenth Amendments (1868, 1870) guaranteed birthright citizenship and the right to vote. But after 1876, Reconstruction came to an end, and powerful white supremacist forces in American society took over ("redeemed") the political system throughout the South, while also claiming cultural and social space.

In the southern states, Jim Crow was a formal system. At its core were laws of segregation that defined people by the color of their skin and kept Black and white people separate in facilities such as parks, schools, hospitals, and transportation. Those facilities provided to African Americans were always of lower quality than those available to white Americans. Both official laws and social practices ensured that this hierarchy stayed in place. Racial discrimination laws economically hindered Black Americans by denying them equal employment, pay, housing, and treatment through the legal system. Voting restrictions like poll taxes and literacy tests were used to exclude them from the political process, perpetuating the system. Rules of social etiquette restricted interactions and constantly reminded African Americans of their inferior status. Those who challenged any elements of this system were subject to extreme violence by both the law and allied paramilitaries like the Ku Klux Klan.[1]

Most of these formal laws and policies were absent in northern states. Instead, Jim Crow in the North took the form of less overt practices such as redlining, a practice of denying loans and other financial services to Black families to keep them out of white areas and to maintain segregated

---

1 For more on the Jim Crow South see Leon Litwack, *Trouble in Mind: Black Southerners in the Age of Jim Crow* (Vintage, 2010). For a focus on experiences in northern states, see Thomas J. Sugrue, *Sweet Land of Liberty: The Forgotten Struggle for Civil Rights in the North* (Random House, 2008). If you can handle accounts of the violence that was a lived reality for many African Americans in this era, read Kidada E. Williams, *They Left Great Marks on Me: African American Testimonies of Racial Violence from Emancipation to World War I* (New York University Press, 2012).

neighborhoods. Violence against African Americans in white areas in the northern states might not have been state-sponsored, but the government and police would still often look the other way when white civilians attacked Black people, including many veterans returning from the First World War, in the bloody "Red Summer" of 1919.

Jim Crow was a discriminatory and violent system that former plantation owners and others tried to justify through a new ideology called **eugenics**. Practitioners of eugenics sought to create a justification for racism using scientific language and ideas to "prove" Black inferiority. In reality, they were distorting science in order to limit Black people's access to resources and to control their labor. It comes as no surprise that their findings benefited the very people who funded their work. Ultimately, the pseudoscience of eugenics helped to lead to the exclusion and ghettoizing of many groups in America, not only African Americans. Ironically, these ideas were closely shared with those who would soon be America's Second World War enemies. In particular, American eugenics was studied by the leaders of Nazi Germany, who applied it to Jews, people with disabilities, Slavs, the Romany people, and others.

Given their treatment, it is almost surprising that African American leaders quickly chose to support the US war effort in 1941. Yet they did. And often, their statements seemed to embrace the freedom and democracy that the United States stood for in principle, if not always in reality. Such important leaders as Dr. Leonidas L. Berry of the African Methodist Episcopal Church called on Black Americans to "fight for the democracy that makes all mankind act, think and feel free."[2] Most African Americans were outraged by the attack on Pearl Harbor. They were hostile to the Japanese plan to—in the words of the *Pittsburgh Courier*—secure "world domination," and some were eager to fight.[3]

Still, before the start of the war, some African Americans had felt an affinity with Japan, which sometimes claimed to be the champion of resistance to European (white) empire. They also faced the reality that even during the war, the racism that had already existed in American society was further heightened by this fight against a non-white enemy. It's worth noting that some African American leaders recognized that the wartime internment of the Japanese American population was closely related to the discrimination and segregation from which they, too, suffered in Jim Crow America.[4] These critics prominently included Margaret Lewis, an editor of the *Afro-American* newspaper, and photographer Charles Williams.

---

2 "A.M.E. Leader Flays Cowardly Japan's Attack," *Pittsburgh Courier*, January 3, 1942.
3 "The World a Part of Asia," *Pittsburgh Courier*, April 25, 1942.
4 Henry Paxton Howard, "Americans in Concentration Camps," *The Crisis*, September 1942, 284.

In general, we should also recognize that African American support for the US war effort was not unconditional. Sometimes, both the Black press and African Americans in military service spoke of their support as contingent on a better future in which they would be able to participate fully in the promises of American society. Also, both were quick to point out the hypocrisy of the US military in recruiting African Americans but then treating them poorly. This contradiction would play an important role in the lives of the Black men and women who served this country during the war, often making vital—but unrecognized—contributions to the eventual victory of the United States and its allies.

AFRICAN AMERICAN AND THE US MILITARY DURING THE SECOND WORLD WAR

The Montford Point Marines, like others who served in the US military, felt a tension between two identities: their identities as Americans and as African Americans. They also fought a double war—against fascism and authoritarianism abroad and against white supremacy and discrimination at home. However, in the long run, the US military also proved to be an important pathway for ending formal racism and segregation in American society. Understanding the African American experience in the military is therefore vital for understanding the struggle against racism in American society more broadly. It's also an important pathway to comprehending the experiences of Black combatants like the Montford Point Marines.

Many Black Americans had served in the US military prior to the Second World War, but their experiences were often mixed at best. In August 1934, the **National Association for the Advancement of Colored People** (NAACP) special counsel Charles Hamilton Houston investigated the conditions of Black soldiers and sailors. He wrote about the bad conditions in which they lived and worked, their exclusion from the Air Corps and Marines, and that they were often restricted to serving as cooks and laborers.[5]

As Europe descended into war in the period from 1939 to 1941, the United States ramped up its war industries. This increase in the production of war materials provided a boom in jobs even before the attack on Pearl Harbor, while the military also expanded in size. However, Jim Crow meant that most of the new, often well-paid industrial jobs initially went to white Americans. Similarly, while white men found new opportunities for jobs, training, and advancement in the military, African Americans were mostly limited to service positions and low ranks, or—as in the case of the Marine Corps—excluded entirely.

---

5 Delmont, *Half American*, 31.

African American leaders saw this situation as further increasing the racial economic divide and believed that the improved economy should benefit all Americans regardless of their race. They were well aware that some officers rejected Black enlistees on flimsy excuses and plantation owners sought exemptions to keep their workers in poorly paid farm jobs rather than letting them join the military or defense industries. Led by A. Philip Randolph, the head of the largest African American labor union at the time, they organized the **March on Washington Movement** in January 1941 to protest this discrimination. A national network of organizers managed to secure massive support and the Black press called on people across the country to join the march. Randolph and others made it clear that they were patriots, but demanded the right to contribute to the war effort as full citizens and as fully compensated workers.

The marchers were in reality appealing to an audience of one: President Franklin Delano Roosevelt. Roosevelt was anxious to avoid a massive march, but also worried that meeting the demands of the protestors would cause a disruption. So while he, as a progressive, probably sympathized with the protestors, he remained cautious. Still, his wife Eleanor Roosevelt and labor advisor Anna M. Rosenberg advised him to meet with Randolph. Roosevelt asked Randolph to call off the march as a precondition to meeting, but Randolph refused. Eventually, Roosevelt agreed to the meeting anyway, and was eventually convinced to issue an executive order prohibiting discrimination in war industries.[6] This order, **Executive Order 8802**, was issued on June 25, 1941.[7] Although written somewhat ambiguously, it was seized upon by the African American leadership as a tool for the longer fight against discrimination. Soon, Black workers were flooding into factories, while Black sailors and soldiers arrived at military training camps across America, both as volunteers and later draftees.

Most of the training camps for the US military were located in the southern states, and Jim Crow was as alive in those camps as it was elsewhere in the South. Many Black recruits found themselves humiliated and beaten daily, restricted to the outskirts of towns, and generally kept away from business districts, stores, and transportation. They were placed in disease-ridden camps with little access to decent conditions, forced to perform menial labor, denied opportunities for advancement, and even abused for wearing the uniforms of their country.[8] Of course, many fought back, but there was little point in complaining. Instead, they wrote letters: to the NAACP, to political officials, to their mothers, and to Black newspapers

---

6 Delmont, *Half American*, 45–63.
7 "Executive Order 8802: Prohibition of Discrimination in the Defense Industry (1941)," National Archives, https://www.archives.gov/milestone-documents/executive-order-8802. (See Document 1 in this book.)
8 Litwack and Postel, *Pearl Harbor Blues*, Chapter 2. Delmont, *Half American*, 65–83.

such as the *Chicago Defender,* the *Pittsburgh Courier,* and the *Baltimore Afro American.*[9] These individuals and organizations did the best they could for those who wrote to them, but conditions hardly improved over the course of the war. The result was devastating and often fatal. Three hundred and twenty sailors and civilians were killed in the **Port Chicago disaster** in California due to unsafe ammunition loading practices and lack of training. State police and white farmers coordinated attacks and manhunts on the African American 94th Engineers during training near Gurdon, Arkansas. Soldiers were beaten by police officers and murdered by civilians. The list of atrocities goes on and on.

African American women who served received similarly discriminatory treatment. Although the Marine Corps did not accept women during the period in which Montford Point Camp was open, other branches of the military did. Of particular note was the 6888th Central Postal Directory Battalion of the United States Army. This segregated unit of 855 African American women helped rectify a vital moral issue: led by their own officers, they rapidly improved the distribution of mail for the European Theater of Operations so that the men serving there could remain in contact with their families at home. But these women faced significant discrimination—they were forbidden from using base facilities like the pool, often shorted in equipment, posted to inferior housing, and held back from promotion in many cases.[10]

The 6888th was just one unit of the approximately 6,500 African American women who served as nurses, clerks, and in other roles in the military during the Second World War. In addition, hundreds of thousands contributed to the war effort by joining important war industries. And then there were the many thousands—like (the future Dr.) Isabell Masters, who appears in this narrative—who put their careers and lives on hold as wives and partners of men who served. They, too, faced discrimination in finding housing near bases and in receiving the benefits due to them.

And yet despite this mistreatment, African Americans would go on to acquit themselves well in the military, both in combat units and in units that formed a significant portion of the logistics system delivering vital materials to the front lines. These soldiers, sailors, Marines, and airmen fought, and they were supported by the Black press and politicians and a largely patriotic civilian community. Ultimately, more than 1.2 million African Americans served in the military during the conflict. They included pilots such as the Tuskegee Airmen, the tankers of the 761st "Black Panther" Tank Battalion in Europe, the men of the 93rd Infantry Division and 24th Infantry Regiment in the Pacific, and crewmen of most of the Navy's

---

9   Many of these letters are reproduced in McGuire, *Taps for a Jim Crow Army.*
10 Priscilla T. Graham, *The Six Triple Eight,* self-published, 2020.

combat and transportation vessels. They also included much of the logistics chain stretched around the world.

However, the African American men and women serving in the military also demanded something in return: that this war would result in their full citizenship and rights. This was the root of the **Double V campaign**, an awareness that victory meant winning against both fascism abroad and discrimination at home. Launched by the *Pittsburgh Courier* in February 1942, the Double V campaign quickly gained massive popularity among African Americans.[11]

The Double V campaign appeared to many observers to be a new idea, but in fact it had deep roots in an awareness by many Black Americans that fighting in America's wars also meant fighting to change America.[12] Frederick Douglass had encouraged African Americans to fight in the Civil War as part of a "double battle" against both slavery in the South and prejudice in the North. W. E. B. Du Bois had hoped that returning veterans from the First World War would liberate the United States just as they had saved democracy in France. Soon, the campaign had been taken up by prominent African American political groups, labor unions, and social organizations. But it was the Black Press that was particularly important, with papers like the *Chicago Defender* and *Pittsburgh Courier* helping to unify the Black community around its aims.

The goals and promise of the Double V campaign helped the NAACP and other Black advocacy organizations grow rapidly during the war, often supported by the men (and women) in the military. By contrast, some white politicians and newspapers accused the Double V campaigners of exploiting the war for political gain. FBI Director J. Edgar Hoover alleged that its proponents were harming the war effort and even implied that they were seditious, or traitors.[13] Certainly, many white Americans saw the campaign as a threat to the segregated and hierarchical America they knew, and it gained little public support or tolerance from the white community.

MONTFORD POINT CAMP AND THE FIRST BLACK MARINES

Initially, the United States Marine Corps did not, in any way, embrace Executive Order 8802. Rather, Corps officers resisted being forced to integrate. The Commandant of the Marine Corps, Major General Thomas Holcomb, was particularly strongly opposed to integration. Defending his

---

11 "The Courier's Double V for a Double Victory Campaign Gets Country-Wide Support," *Pittsburgh Courier*, February 14, 1942. (See Document 3 in this book.)
12 Delmont, *Half American*, 102–103.
13 Delmont, *Half American*, 106.

objection before the General Board of the US Navy, Holcomb argued that "there would be a definite loss of efficiency in the Marine Corps if we have to take Negroes . . . the Negro race has every opportunity now to satisfy its aspirations for combat, in the Army—a very much larger organization than the Navy or Marine Corps—and their desire to enter the naval service is largely, I think, to break into a club *that doesn't want them.*" He also declared that "If it were a question of having a Marine Corps of 5,000 Whites or 250,000 Negroes, *I would rather have the whites.*"[14] Holcomb and the Corps were nevertheless forced to bend before the will of President Roosevelt. After nearly a year of opposition, they accepted the enlistment of the first Black Marines on May 14, 1942.

Still, having been forced to accept Black recruits into his formerly exclusively white Corps, Holcomb then acted to ensure that they would be confined to subservient roles. As described by historian (and Marine) Cameron McCoy, he issued a secret order to the white officers charged with training and leading the new Black personnel on May 14, 1943. Known as **Letter of Instruction no. 421**, its contents were kept hidden from both African American recruits and Holcomb's superiors in the War Department.[15]

Briefly, Letter of Instruction no. 421 ensured that the admission of Black Marines would not upset the overall racial order of white supremacy. "At no time," the order read, "shall there be colored noncommissioned officers senior to white men in the same unit." In other words, no Black Marine would give an order to a white Marine. The letter also controlled and limited the promotion of Black Marines and required that the rolls kept of Marine Corps units clearly list Black personnel separately.

Montford Point Camp was key to this strategy of limiting and segregating Black Marines. It was founded, quite simply, to ensure that Black Marines would be trained in a tightly controlled, segregated manner.[16] It would have been easier, logistically, to simply send Black enlistees to the existing training camps in San Diego, California, and Parris Island, South Carolina—but this option was rejected in order to separate them from the white Marines.

---

14 Maj. Gen. Thomas Holcomb testimony in Hearings of the General Board of the Navy, 23 January 1942. Subject: "Enlistment of Men of Colored Race (201)," Operational Archives Branch, Naval Historical Center, 18.
15 Letter from the Commandant, US Marine Corps, to All Commanding Officers, May 14, 1943, Subject: Colored Personnel (formerly classified CONFIDENTIAL), Record Group 127: Records of the United States Marine Corps, History and Museums Division, PUBLICATION BACKGROUND FILES, "Brief History of Blacks in USMC, 1942–73," Draft Text & Source Documents, Box 135 (US National Archives and Records Administration) (see Document 2 in this book). See also McCoy, "Mr. President," 68–75.
16 Memorandum from the Director, Division of Plans and Policies, to the Commandant, US Marine Corps, February 25, 1942. Subject: Enlistment of the colored race other than in the messman branch (Historical Reference Branch, History Division, USMC).

Montford Point was not only separate from these two principal Marine Corps training bases. It was also unequal. The conditions at the camp are vividly depicted in Part I, but it's worth outlining them here. The location was a barely cleared forest with some pre-existing facilities used by the Civilian Conservation Corps. These included a few headquarters buildings and 120 prefabricated **Homasote** huts, each designed to hold 16 men (but sometimes holding many more).[17] The huts were decaying already, and it would be some time before metal **Quonset** huts were added to the camp. Training facilities like the rifle range were rough, and those that were more elaborate were shared with white Marines and could only rarely be used by the Montford Pointers. The food preparation, water, and sanitary facilities were substandard and unhealthy.[18] There was initially no provision for the Marine recruits—or "boots"—to use the nearby established combat training sites that formed the existing Camp Lejeune facilities for white Marines.

The first African American recruits arrived on August 26, 1942. Most of the early "boots" were volunteers, but beginning in January 1943 many were draftees through the Selective Service System. It's important to note that almost all of the African Americans who joined the Marine Corps did so without mentorship, guidance, or a family connection to the Corps. A few exceptions, including First Sergeant Jack McDowell, followed older brothers into the service.

The majority of the new enlistees were from the northern states, and some of these were unprepared for the realities of formal segregation and shocked by camp conditions. Recruits from the southern states were, of course, more used to the legalized and formal segregation of Jim Crow.[19] Partly for these reasons, the initial recruiting drives in 1942 particularly targeted the southern states. Yet for perhaps the very same reasons, African Americans from the South did not enlist in the Corps in the expected numbers.[20] Still, they made up a good proportion of the men who passed through Montford Point. In their interviews with historians like Melton McLaurin, these men generally report that they were less surprised than the northerners by the harsh treatment at camp and in the surrounding towns. In particular, they knew to expect that their uniforms would buy them little of the goodwill enjoyed by white Marines.

The Montford Pointers initially had white officers and drill instructors as their leaders. This was both by design and necessity, as there were no

---

17 Nalty, *The Right to Fight*, 5.
18 See page 44 of this book.
19 McCoy, "Jim Crow America and the Marines of Montford Point in the World War II Era," 52–88.
20 Nalty, *The Right to Fight*, 2.

Black Marines to serve in either capacity at the beginning. Later, Black drill instructors would be chosen from among the recruits, although (as already mentioned) the officer corps remained exclusively white until after the end of the Second World War.

The experience of the "boots" at Montford Point was one of ceaseless movement and exhaustion.[21] Some veterans, looking back on these experiences, also remember abuse at the hands of officers and drill instructors. Unlike the overall conditions, however, this treatment may have been more the result of a callous military training culture than overt racism. Certainly, the Black drill instructors and noncommissioned officers appointed after January 1943 are remembered as being equally brutal and relentless as the white ones.[22] In fact, African American sergeants like Edgar R. Huff and Gilbert H. "Hashmark" Johnson may have been even tougher on the recruits than their white predecessors, knowing that the Black recruits had to achieve excellence in order to be accepted in a white Corps.[23]

And it should be noted that many of the recruits also have good memories of Montford Point Camp. They remember having fun with friends and platoon-mates, playing practical jokes on each other or just sitting around and talking. Some also remember the three square meals and the satisfaction of learning to fire a rifle or manage a big gun, or even just getting in shape. Training was initially intensely physical in order to prepare the recruits for the rigors of war. Perhaps the most dangerous of the exercises was learning to climb up and down the landing nets that would connect ships to landing craft once they reached the Pacific Islands that were their objective. The first fatality among the Montford Pointers, Corporal Gilbert Fraser Jr., was killed while practicing on these nets. The remaining men soon named the central road in the camp Fraser Road in his honor.

After initial conditioning, the men also learned to become riflemen by spending a great amount of time on the range. Initially, the weapon they trained on was the bolt-action M1903 Springfield standard issue rifle. Those who passed the range qualified as "marksmen." If they excelled and earned "sharpshooter" or "expert" qualifications, they received extra pay.

---

21   Culp, *First Black United States Marines*, 44–65. Culp takes pains to justify the treatment of the "boots" as necessary for preparing men for battle.
22   See Culmer's account in this book. The first three Black NCOs were appointed in January 1943, with nineteen more following in February. Shaw and Donnelly, *Blacks in the Marine Corps*, 10–11.
23   This claim is often repeated by the veterans interviewed in this project and was corroborated by Johnson himself in 1967 remarks to the Camp Lejeune Chapter of the Montford Point Marine Association. Sergeant Major Gilbert H. Johnson remarks, Camp Lejeune Chapter, MPMA, in Negro Marines, Subject File, Reference Section, History & Music Division, Headquarters of the Marine Corps, 1967. Shaw and Donnelly, *Blacks in the Marine Corps*, 12.

Unlike white Marines, the Montford Pointers did not, however, receive training in other weapons such as hand grenades or rocket launchers, because they were not initially intended for front-line combat units.[24] Technically, like all Marines, they could also apply to be specialists in all sorts of occupation areas from radio to engineering. Suspiciously, only very few of them ever qualified for these desirable appointments.[25]

The Marines sometimes resisted the harsh treatment they received while at camp. One "boot" actually fired at a group of officers after some abuse. Yet such violent resistance was rare.[26] Still, there was plenty of collective protest. In one famous event called the Death March, a class of recruits was forced to run around the camp after evidence was found that one had used his bayonet to pull away some of the crumbling material of his hut. When they reached Fraser Road, however, they began to refuse to go any further. Instead, they allegedly rushed to the "brig" (jail) and demanded that they all be arrested. The event became a source of pride for the Marines who participated and a legend told to those who came after them.[27]

The towns that surrounded Montford Point were reportedly even worse than the training camp itself. Some African American enlistees, just arrived from New York or Chicago, found a rude awakening in the depth and extent of discrimination in the Jim Crow South.[28] These experiences often had already begun during their journey to the camp, since segregation was legal south of the Mason–Dixon line. Petty aggressions and systemic discrimination also affected the "boots" every time they went into nearby towns. The town closest to the camp was Jacksonville, North Carolina. Entirely segregated, it was not very welcoming to the new enlistees. While there were a few Black-owned businesses where they could get a drink or sundries, white-owned businesses were sites of danger, where a poorly chosen word or a minor disagreement could result in violence. The buses to and from town were also perilous. Municipal bus drivers sometimes ignored or even ejected the Montford Pointers. Black recruits were usually on their own in the face of this treatment, without institutional support. Some remember being aided by white Marines, or their own officers, but usually they had to choose whether to bend to the situation or face the repercussions and dangers on their own.[29] Many adopted the

---

24 Culp, *First Black United States Marines*, 60–61.
25 See, for instance, page 69 in this book.
26 Mclaurin, *Marines of Montford Point*, 105.
27 Nalty, *The Right to Fight*, 15.
28 See McCoy, "Jim Crow America and the Marines of Montford Point in the World War II Era," 26–51. For example, Norman R. Payne, interviewed by Melton A. McLaurin, July 14, 2004, http://library.uncw.edu/web/montford/transcripts/Payne_Norman.html.
29 McLaurin, *Marines of Montford Point*, 96–117. See also the oral histories represented in Part I: The Graphic History in this book.

strategy of traveling in large groups[30] while others avoided setting foot in the nearby towns, instead heading north to Washington, DC, when they had leave.[31]

Despite the obstacles they faced, the vast majority of the Montford Point "boots" made it through training and looked forward to posting overseas. But what would they do there? The original intent of the Corps Commandant was that Black Marines would be held in service roles. As a result, most of the Montford Pointers who served during the Second World War were officially enlisted into the sixty-three depot and ammunition companies. These were labor units intended to manage stores of materials for white combat outfits. The Corps also trained African Americans for servitor roles that they had traditionally been allowed in the Navy, including a Mess Attendant School and Officers' Cooks and Stewards Schools—postings that were not generally seen as desirable by the recruits.[32]

Other Montford Pointers were formed into units that were technically designated as combat-ready: the 51st and 52nd Composite Defense Battalions. The main role of these units was to hold territory already captured against possible enemy counterattacks by air or sea. These men received additional training in antiaircraft and antishipping artillery.[33] However, the members of the first of these units—the 51st—were initially placed into the reserves rather than recognized as regular members of the Corps. Similarly, the unit was initially placed on "inactive" duty.[34] The 51st was fortunate in its initial commander, Samuel A. Woods Jr., who made sure that the men were still ready for combat. A South Carolinian, Woods was not free of racism, but his prejudice primarily found expression through paternalism. He treated the Black Marines as if he were their father, earned the respect of many of them, and argued that they were competent to serve in combat.[35] Perhaps because of this attitude, he was replaced by the much less effective Lt. Colonel Curtis W. Legette once the unit was sent overseas.[36]

---

30 McLaurin, *Marines of Montford Point* 83, 185.
31 Averet Corley, interviewed by Melton A. McLaurin, July 23, 2004, http://library.uncw.edu/web/montford/transcripts/Corley_Averet.html.
32 Shaw and Donnelly, *Blacks in the Marine Corps*, 10.
33 Culp, *First Black United States Marines*, 90–96.
34 Department of the Navy, "Marines Announce Plans for Recruiting African-Americans," Department of the Navy, May 20, 1942, Record Group 428: General Records of the Department of the Navy, 1941–2004 (US National Archives and Records Administration), reproduced in McCoy, "Jim Crow America and the Marines of Montford Point in the World War II Era," 162.
35 Nalty, *Right to Fight*, 6; McCoy, "Jim Crow America and the Marines of Montford Point in the World War II Era," 21.
36 Culp, *First Black United States Marines*, 130. The replacement may have partly been the result of incidents that took place in camp, but LeGette is remembered as being arrogant and disdainful toward the men he commanded.

MONTFORD POINTERS IN THE PACIFIC THEATER OF OPERATIONS

Once they left Montford Point Camp, the Montford Pointers' experiences became part of the larger war effort in the Pacific. Here they encountered both new obstacles and new opportunities to work through the tension between their American and African American identities.

The **Pacific Theater of Operations** (or War in the Pacific) is the name military historians assign to one major part of the Second World War. For the United States, this conflict began with the Japanese bombing of the US naval base at Pearl Harbor on December 7, 1941, an attack famously described by President Franklin Delano Roosevelt as "a day that will live in infamy." But the origins of the war are much deeper. The Japanese state, late to industrialize compared to its European and US rivals, and also short on resources, spent much of the late nineteenth and early twentieth centuries acquiring islands such as Iwo Jima, Okinawa, and Taiwan, and expanding into the Korean Peninsula and then China. Chinese forces fought back, and the United States denied resources to Japan and provided some aid to China. The Japanese Army wanted to continue to focus on conquering China, but the powerful Navy believed that Japan could only get the resources it needed by defeating the United States.

The attack on Pearl Harbor was just one step in a concerted effort by Japan to dominate the Pacific. It was followed, in early 1942, by Japanese forces landed on Wake Island, Guam, and the Philippines. Japanese armies also invaded British colonies in Malaya and elsewhere. Their forces soon annexed independent Thailand (Siam), British-controlled Burma, French Indochina, and Dutch possessions in Indonesia. Together, these new colonies provided fuel, rubber, and the other vital materials Japan needed. The Japanese military also built a ring of fortifications and jumping-off points across the Pacific. Often, the Japanese claimed to be "liberating" Asian and Pacific Islander populations from foreign control, but very soon their rule proved to be authoritarian and extractive.

Arrayed against the Japanese was a huge international force. Foremost were the massive but poorly trained and equipped Chinese army and its allied units. There were also British Empire contingents that included forces from Australia, India, and even West Africa. Philippine and Vietnamese guerilla forces harried the Japanese. But perhaps the heaviest load in men and material was carried by the United States. US Naval forces stopped Japanese expansion in the Battle of Midway in June 1942, and soon after American and Australian soldiers halted them in New Guinea. By 1943, these allied units were moving forward. Backed by the industrial power of the US economy, they pushed back a Japanese military that was increasingly weakened by submarine and air attacks on their supply lines. Throughout 1944 and into 1945, US Marines and army units conducted a campaign of seizing key islands in the Pacific while the Navy and its airmen sank major assets of the Japanese fleet.[37]

Although not initially allowed by the Corps to join the fighting, thousands of Montford Pointers soon came under fire—and shot back. This happened in two ways. First, many of the Pacific Islands were full of mountainous jungles and difficult to clear entirely of the enemy. Thus both Depot Companies and the composite defense battalions were engaged in mopping-up operations and faced guerilla warfare conditions throughout the war.[38] These units took the long train West to San Diego starting in August 1943, and from there boarded ships bound for the Hawaiian Islands. From there, they were posted to conquered islands like Noumea in New Caledonia and Funafuti in the Ellice Islands, where they managed ammunition and supplies going onward to frontline units. Often, these islands had been incompletely cleared and they faced mines, traps, and sporadic gunfights.

Second, invasion planners quickly found that it was necessary to support landing forces with immediate access to ammunition and other supplies. Thus members of the ammunition companies soon found themselves in the first waves of landings on the islands Saipan, Tinian, Peleliu, and Iwo Jima.[39] These were bloody fights and in many cases Montford Pointers found themselves under heavy artillery bombardment and in intense firefights as soon as they landed.

When battle wasn't imminent, the Montford Pointers spent most of their time laboring on, living, and occupying islands behind the front line, either doing logistical work or training or waiting for the next fight. And again, many of these memories of their time include pleasant interludes in camp with their friends, or on liberty leave in local communities. Then, at the end of the war, they found themselves participating in the occupation of Japan. Some were also briefly sent to supply areas of North China previously occupied by the Japanese.[40]

What was service in the Pacific like for these African American Marines? The campaign against Japan brought diverse populations into contact with each other during a period in which the established hierarchies and rules of race were being challenged. An Asian empire, for a time,

---

37 For a useful and up-to-date history of the conflict see Clifford J. Rodgers, Ty Seidule, and Steve R. Waddell, eds., *The West Point History of World War II*, two volumes (Simon & Schuster, 2015–2016). See also Waldo Heinrichs and Marc Gallicchio, *Implacable Foes: War in the Pacific, 1944–1945* (Oxford University Press, 2017).
38 Culp, *First Black United States Marines*, 133–138, 188–190.
39 Culp, *First Black United States Marines*, 139–187, 194–204.
40 Shaw and Donnelly, *Blacks in the Marine Corps*, 42–44.

defeated the established European powers. Recruits from all over the world were finding themselves in this theater of operations, including West African soldiers fighting for Britain, Filipino resisters allied with the United States, and Korean conscripts led by Japanese officers. In this mix, African American soldiers, sailors, and Marines found themselves in a complex position. One revealing story even tells of a young African American soldier asking that his gravestone read "Here lies a black man, killed fighting a yellow man for the protection of a white man."[41]

There may be a certain truth to this story, even if the particulars are made up. African American soldiers and Marines often found themselves posted on islands that had once been ruled by Europeans, but then conquered by the Japanese. Could they help but reflect on Japanese victories as a challenge to white supremacy? Similarly, many Black servicemen were posted to Australia and New Zealand, where they were sometimes treated by the white populations with less racism than in their own hometowns.[42] Would this not have raised questions in their minds about why they could not expect similar treatment at home? Finally, many Black servicemen served in units with white officers and faced significant discrimination. Even Army units with African American officers found themselves deprived of important materials or placed in the worst assignments. Might this not have caused them to wonder whether it was worth serving this country that did not treat them as equals?[43]

Yet service in the Pacific may have challenged the racist order in America in another, more subtle, but even more important way. Many Black Marines reported the strange camaraderie of moments under fire, when at least for a while, there was no race. This experience mirrored that of African Americans fighting in Europe.[44] After battle, white and Black Marines would share cigarettes and stillness. Others also remembered the surprise of experiencing acceptance, and even praise, from their fellow white Marines. Admittedly, this experience wasn't always uncomplicated. Reuben McNair, who carried ammunition to the front line and was wounded during the bloody battle of Peleliu, remembers white Marines saying "the black angels saved us." But he didn't get an entirely warm and fuzzy feeling from the thanks they gave. "It wasn't like when James Brown comes along singing I'm black and I'm proud. . . . At that particular time, we felt a little uncomfortable."[45] Also, such moments usually passed quickly and

---

41 Neil A. Wynn, "The Impact of the Second World War on the American Negro," *Journal of Contemporary History* 6 (1971): 49.
42 This is not to ignore these countries' own significant problems with racism.
43 See Dixon, *African Americans and the Pacific War, 1941–1945*.
44 This phenomenon is discussed in Guglielmo, *Divisions*, 328–334.
45 McLaurin, *Marines of Montford Point*, 127–128.

were replaced by the normal hierarchy soon after the end of fighting. Still, their acceptance as Marines, even if only temporary and within the brotherhood of combat, was a crack in the system of segregation and hierarchy that defined Jim Crow America.

THE TENSION OF MASCULINITY

The historical context of the Montford Point Marines highlights an important element of the African American experience that was first enunciated by the sociologist and historian W. E. B. Du Bois—the idea of a double consciousness. Du Bois wrote in 1903 that "One feels his two-ness,—an American, a Negro; two souls, two thoughts, two unreconciled strivings; two warring ideals in one dark body, whose dogged strength alone keeps it from being torn asunder."[46] In this way, the first Black Marines had to reconcile serving American interests in an American military through a patriotic national lens with the real experience of being treated as inferior members of that military.

In order to grasp how Montford Pointers experienced this tension, we also have to consider how they understood what it meant to be men and to be masculine. Like other African Americans serving in the Pacific, they had to confront two seemingly contradictory racist stereotypes of Black men that were deeply entrenched in American culture at the time. The first one portrayed them as docile, timid, or cowardly. The second depicted them as brutish and uncivilized. Both stereotypes had their roots in the slave regime as well as Jim Crow, but they also had a special value during the Second World War. Those who opposed civil rights for African Americans knew that recognizing them as fine soldiers, sailors, and Marines meant a step toward equality. As one Black lawyer and educator wrote to Secretary of War Henry L. Stimson:

> In the Army the Negro is taught to be a man, a fighting man; in brief, a soldier. It is impossible to create a dual personality which will be on the one hand a fighting man toward the foreign enemy, and on the other, a craven who will accept treatment as less than equal at home.[47]

Of course, the question of Black military service was very much a racial question, but it was also a gender question. During this war, Americans solidified an already developing sense of what it meant to be masculine. They came to think of both America itself, and its ideal men, as muscular and

---

[46] W. E. B. Du Bois, *The Souls of Black Folk*, Chicago, 1903, edited by David W. Blight and Robert Gooding-Williams (Bedford Books, 1997), 38.
[47] William Hastie, "Survey and Recommendations Concerning the Integration of the Negro Soldier into the Army," submitted to the Secretary of the Army, September 22, 1941. Dixon, *African Americans and the Pacific War*, 178.

virile.[48] The Marines in particular exuded an air of heightened masculinity, and many of the future Montford Pointers picked up on it. Many report a strong sense of admiration for the image of masculinity embodied by Marines: for the tall and muscular men they saw marching in the streets, their smart uniforms, and their elite reputation.

At the same time, America demanded smart, compassionate officers who could inspire those who fought and the country at large. This was an even more elite masculinity of leadership.

African American servicemen like the Montford Pointers thus fought two successive battles to be recognized: first as men, and then as men capable of being officers. First, they had to fight to be recognized as fit to serve in a man's military role at all. Initially, many Marine officers believed that African Americans lacked the ability to be courageous and capable soldiers. It was to overcome this prejudiced attitude among officers that the first Black drill instructors constantly told the men they were training that they had to be *better Marines* than the white recruits: stronger, better shots, more physically fit. Yet no matter their achievements, once in the combat zone, most of the African American Marines were still not seen as manly enough for combat. Instead, they were placed into service units designated as Depot or Ammunition Companies. The only full-fledged combat units made up of Montford Pointers were the two composite defense battalions, which were assigned to already-conquered islands. Of course, Black Marines quickly did find themselves in combat, but that was not the Corps' intent! In fact, as late as the first campaigns in Korea, most Black Marines would still initially be posted to Graves Registration and other service units. Only later did they become integrated into frontline rifle companies.

Beyond the battle to be recognized as men who could endure combat, Black Marines also had to fight to be recognized as men who were capable of leadership. In this fight, African American soldiers and sailors made important progress during the war. Across the Army and Navy, over 7,000 African Americans managed to reach officer rank during the war, transforming both of those branches of service. The first African American General, Benjamin O. Davis, was also named during the war. In the Marine Corps, however, opposition to Black officers remained strong. This opposition rested on the assertion that they were not the right kind of *men*—not the type of leader you would want for other men. The first African American officer in the corps, Frederick Branch, was only made a Second Lieutenant—the very lowest officer rank—on November 10, 1945. The war was already over at this point. The second such officer would only be named in 1949. This battle—the battle to be seen as worthy of being officers—thus became part of the longer struggle for civil rights in America.

---

48   Christina S. Jarvis, *The Male Body at War: American Masculinity during World War II* (Northern Illinois University Press, 2010).

LOOKING BOTH FORWARD AND BACKWARD

The African Americans who served in the Second World War joined for many reasons, but at least some of them saw the war as a fight to achieve their own rights. This is evident in numerous statements of the men who enlisted, including those interviewed for this project. African American newspapers like the *Chicago Defender* also expressed this motivation, arguing that "Negroes CAN and MUST profit from the discipline that war will impose on all American citizens and BEGIN NOW under a planned program to secure all of the things which have previously been denied."[49]

The Black press knew well that sharing stories of African Americans in the military was key to making a case for changes in the status of all Black people after the war. Unfortunately, most American media of the time downplayed the role of African Americans in the war effort. More than a 1.2 million Black soldiers, sailors, and airmen served in the US Armed Forces during this conflict, but they rarely featured in Hollywood wartime productions or the pages of newspapers like the *News of the World* or *The New York Times* and magazines like *Life*. The few officially produced films that did acknowledge their service had to wait until late in the war, when the US government finally allowed leftist filmmaker Frank Capra to make *The Negro Soldier* (1944).[50] The Navy-focused follow-up *The Negro Sailor* (1945) came a year later.[51]

Of course, the African American press did not let this omission go unchallenged. In February 1944 an editorial in *The Crisis*, the newspaper of the National Association for the Advancement of Colored People (NAACP), complained that white people might "get the impression Negroes are doing little if anything to win the victory."[52] In response, the Black press was very active in trying to spread the stories of African Americans in service as well as supporting their struggles for justice while in the military. Yet America still did not have much time for these stories, which continued to receive little coverage in the mainstream press.

These efforts to highlight the contributions of Black servicemen and women was one exercise of the emerging civil rights movement. As the war came to an end, a much-enlarged Black press and vastly expanded NAACP

---

49 "Ask Scope of Defense Bias Probe," *Chicago Defender*, July 19, 1941; "Davis Finally Replies To Request For A Negro On War Labor Board," *Chicago Defender*, March 28, 1942. McCoy, "Jim Crow America and the Marines of Montford Point in the World War II Era," 38.
50 Carlton Moss, *The Negro Soldier*, directed by Frank Capra, War Activities Committee of the Motion Picture Industry, 1944.
51 Department of the Navy, *The Negro Sailor*, directed by Henry Levin, US Navy Motion Films Production, 1945.
52 "Omissions from Newsreels" and "Along the NAACP Battlefront," *The Crisis*, February 1944, 39, 51–52. Dixon, *African Americans and the Pacific War*, 9.

led increasing calls for an end to segregation and inequality. Returning veterans quickly took up key roles in this movement. With a few exceptions, these organizations had followed a "realistic" strategy during the war. They hoped that they could gradually gain key concessions from the government and slowly change American society without a dangerous disruption.[53]

Yet upon returning home after the war, Black Marines still encountered a country that was far from ready to recognize their service, let alone undergo the kind of transformations that African Americans were clamoring for. While some were able to benefit from the GI Bill education benefits and Veteran Administration home and business loans theoretically offered to all returning veterans, others found themselves stymied by local government officials who delayed and denied them the benefits they had earned.[54] Numerous Montford Point veterans were also harassed or attacked for "impersonating a Marine." The most famous such case was Sergeant Major Edgar Huff, the much-storied drill instructor who was falsely incarcerated in Atlanta, had his papers torn up in front of his face, and was even abandoned by a Marine Captain who arrived to retrieve some drunken white Marines.[55] Meanwhile, although a series of senior noncommissioned Black Marine officers were finally allowed to enter Officer Candidate School, only one—Frederick C. Branch—successfully became an officer in 1945, and then only because he agreed to go on inactive duty right away. The next year, additional Black Marines were similarly commissioned, but only as reserve officers on inactive status.[56]

By 1946, in fact, there were few Black veterans left in a Marine Corps that was rapidly decreasing in size and whose leaders envisioned a much smaller proportion of African Americans than in the other branches.[57] Most of those who remained were directed into Depot Companies and the Stewards' Branch. It was pressure from outside the military that transformed the situation inside the military. Specifically, President Harry S. Truman, in 1948, issued **Executive Order 9981**, legally declaring equality of treatment within the military regardless of race, color, or national origin. He did this because he was mired in a difficult re-election campaign in which Black voters were pivotal. The effects of Executive Order 9981 were not widespread, although some Montford Pointers—including at least one featured in this graphic narrative—quickly found themselves in

---

53 Lee Finkle, "The Conservative Aims of Militant Rhetoric: Black Protest during World War II," *Journal of American History* (60), 1973, 692–713.
54 Because these systems were decentralized, veterans could have very different experiences based on their region and the attitudes of local officials. See Delmont 266–270; Guglielmo 374–377; Morehouse 202–207.
55 McCoy, "Mr. President, what of the Marines?," 176–177.
56 Shaw and Donnelly, *Blacks in the Marine Corps*, 48.
57 Shaw and Donnelly, *Blacks in the Marine Corps*, 49.

integrated battalions (although still segregated companies). One side effect of the desegregation of training facilities following Truman's Executive Order was the deactivation of Montford Point Camp itself on September 9, 1949. The veterans featured in this book remember that event as both sweet and bitter at the same time, marking a step forward in integration but also the end of an era.

Still, it was not until the Korean War that Black Marines would finally serve in truly integrated combat units. The war imposed huge and sudden demands for manpower. Consequently, Black veterans of the Second World War were called back and almost immediately integrated individually into otherwise all-white units that were thrust into combat in the worst conditions. Anecdotal evidence suggests that these circumstances of "foxhole integration" in the face of enemy fire made the desegregation process easier. Marine officers like Major General Oliver P. Smith and Colonel Homer A. Litzberg Jr. echo our own interviewees when recalling that in general, there was little objection to the arrival of small groups of Black Marines.[58] But their numbers remained small, and with the disappearance of all-Black units, there was no attempt at formal record-keeping of racial issues.

In fact, it would still take decades for Black Marines to feel like they received truly equal treatment to match their equal legal status. Systemic racism was still embedded in the tests that put "boots" into different specializations and determined who might advance in rank. Individual officers, NCOs, and Marines still sometimes discriminated against their Black peers.[59] In fact, as the civil rights movement and the fight against racial discrimination accelerated in the 1960s, incidents of racial discrimination and strife became more widespread, especially at the training facility at Camp Lejeune—just across from the former site of Montford Point.[60] Similarly, oral histories from among the approximately 41,000 Black servicemen and women (including Marines) who served in Vietnam reveal plenty of discrimination.[61] Statistics also show a higher-than-average Black fatality rate early in the war. While technically not the result of formal policies, they often nevertheless constituted a form of systemic racism. These experiences also contributed to high levels of anti-war sentiment among African Americans who served.

Yet as indicated by many of the Montford Pointers interviewed for this book, in many ways the Corps had now moved *ahead* of American society as a whole. While Americans were fighting and dying in Korea and Vietnam,

---

58 Shaw and Donnelly, *Blacks in the Marine Corps*, 59.
59 McCoy, "Mr. President, What of the Marines?," 227–240.
60 See House Armed Services Committee, *Inquiry into the Disturbances at Marine Core Base, Camp Lejeune, N.C., on July 20, 1969* (Washington, DC, December 15, 1969).
61 Wallace Terry, *Bloods: Black Veterans of the Vietnam War: An Oral History* (Presidio, 1965).

the civil rights movement was facing great opposition at home. Significant progress was only made very slowly. Black Second World War veterans like Hosea Williams, Amzie More, and Medgar Evers found that they had returned home from war to wage a new campaign for their rights at home.[62] Montford Pointers were among the campaigners. Perhaps the most famous was Cecil B. Moore. As a lawyer, president of the Philadelphia NAACP, and later Philadelphia city councilman, Moore tirelessly fought against discrimination in housing, jobs, and schooling. Of course, not every African American Marine veteran became as involved in the struggle, but they all had to deal with a society in which race and racism remained a powerful feature. Some Black veterans struggled with receiving the benefits promised to them in the form of the GI Bill, which the government had passed to provide pathways for returning servicepeople to enter the middle class. Has the situation improved since 1942? Some of the Montford Pointers featured in this project believe that it has, but others are not so sure.

What the veterans did agree on was the value of their brotherhood for each other and the potential of the support and mentorship they might provide for future generations of Black Marines. In 1965, a group of Montford Pointers living in the Philadelphia area, including Moore as well as Master Sergeant Brooke E. Gray, organized a reunion for those they had served with. In the end, over 400 veterans attended this event. By the next year, a National Montford Point Marine Association (NMPMA) had been formed and eleven chapters started across the country. Over time, Montford Pointers across the country established forty-seven chapters and a "Ladies Auxiliary." The organizers initially focused on "promot[ing] and [preserving] the strong bonds of friendship" among the Montford Pointers, but this mission expanded quickly. Many of the members focused on projects to provide financial safety nets and moral support to their fellows as well as social programs aimed at youths and other veterans.[63] These programs still exist today. The NMPMA has also provided plenty of support for new generations of young Black Marines and other servicemen and women, who in turn now provide aid to the remaining Montford Pointers, most of whom are now in their nineties.

The NMPMA also works to share the stories and lessons of the Montford Point Marines, and they are an important partner in this project. While many of the veterans initially found it difficult to talk about their experiences, even with their families, others have been working hard to share their experiences and their wisdom. This is the desire that motivated the creation of this book, and achieving it is the goal of this graphic narrative.

---

62 Delmont, *Half American*, xv.
63 See History, Purpose, and Constitution and Bylaws of the National Montford Point Marine Association. Herman Smalls Rhett, "The Montford Point Marines: Final Roll Call," unpublished, revised edition, 2008.

PART IV
ORAL HISTORY: APPLYING A RESEARCH METHODOLOGY

When a historian has a research question that they want to find an answer to, their research methodology determines how they gather evidence that can lead them to this answer. Often, the term "research" is used to cover the whole process of finding those answers—from reading the background material other scholars have produced all the way to interpreting the primary sources to arrive at the answers. In this section, however, we are using the term "research" to focus on how we approached our primary evidence—the oral histories of the veterans at the heart of this project.

ORAL HISTORY AS METHOD

Historians usually think of oral history as a set of practices by which scholars can recover the eyewitness evidence of events and experiences that happened in the past. Emerging in the first part of the twentieth century but really taking hold in the 1960s, oral history gained popularity partly as a way to challenge historians' traditional emphasis on powerful people and their actions. Most of the evidence available about the past in written form, and collected in archives, provides the perspectives of kings, generals, and diplomats. However, in this decade, a new generation of historians, driven in part by global trends of decolonization, feminism, and anti-racism, became interested in the experiences of people who are normally excluded from these archives. They realized that by interviewing living people, they could get information about the lives of women, people of color, the working class, and others whose histories were excluded from traditional archives.

At first, there were few rules for collecting and interpreting oral histories through interviews, which were often conducted haphazardly. But practitioners quickly began to figure out best practices for doing this work accurately, effectively, and ethically. They formed organizations and shared this information with each other. Today, there are professional groups such as the Oral History Association, the USC Shoah Foundation, and—particularly important in terms of veterans' oral histories—the Library of Congress Veterans History Project.[1]

The guidelines provided by these groups emphasize several core principles. The first is that the historian is "collecting" the account of a human being about their own past and about those around them. So the process must be shaped by an ethical commitment to the individuals involved. These participants must consent to participating, must be made as comfortable as possible, and should be able to communicate the meaning they see in their own stories—especially if they are members of vulnerable communities. Their rights must be protected by the researcher, including at times a right to privacy, but oral history narrators should generally be identified. Normally, it is best practice to obtain formal permission both for the interview and for any recording. This permission will often take the shape of a formal signed legal release form.

An additional principle in the methodology for oral history is that the interview is based on a relationship between the interviewer and the narrator. At all times, the historian needs to be aware of the way in which their own actions and behaviors, the setting of the interview, the questions they ask, and how they react to answers might affect the narrator or shape the narrative. The interviewer also has to consider how their relationship to the narrator and their community may affect the interview. For example, interviewing your own grandmother has both advantages and disadvantages compared to interviewing someone from a community of which you are not a member.

Oral histories are most useful when they are available to a broad audience, although there are rare exceptions in which they must be kept partly or fully confidential to protect living people. Because both the narrator and the researcher usually want to share an oral history accurately and widely, it is usually best to record them, often through video or audio. Deciding which recording method and equipment to use is just one step in preparing for the interview. The oral historian also needs to research the topics they will address and, if possible, anything they can learn about the individual. Then they need to prepare the narrator for the interview, but do so carefully. Any preparation will help the narrator become more comfortable and give complete answers, but it might also cause the narrator to shape their answers in order to meet what they perceive to be the interests of the narrator. It is also sometimes useful to ask the narrator to bring pictures or objects that might help them to tell their story.

---

1 Oral History Association "Best Practices," https://oralhistory.org/best-practices/; USC Shoah Foundation, "Interviewer Guidelines," 2021, https://sfi.usc.edu/content/interviewer-guidelines; Library of Congress, "VHP Field Kit," https://www.loc.gov/programs/veterans-history-project/how-to-participate/vhp-field-kit/ (all accessed April 30, 2024).

A historian might conduct only one interview or many with the same person. Some social researchers believe that three interviews are preferable, but it really depends on the purpose and setting of the project and the availability and needs of the narrator.[2] Usually, interviews should be kept relatively short, with the comfort of the narrator as a key measure of length. In any case, the interviewer should make sure to agree on these details with the narrator ahead of the interview.

Preparation for an interview also requires the development of questions. Generally, the interviewer will begin by asking some identifying questions and follow these with a series of open-ended questions. The main point of the questions in an oral history project is to help the narrator tell their story, rather than to get specific factual answers. There are a variety of techniques for getting full answers that really represent the narrator's experiences. One is to begin simply by asking the narrator to tell you a story about something. Another is to ask superficial factual questions followed by deep and open-ended questions. Still another is to give the narrator something to respond to—some quotes or physical objects, for example. The success of each approach depends very much on the individual narrator.

Finally, once an oral history is completed, it should be preserved somehow. It should generally be made available to the public, but the researcher has a special obligation to ensure that members of the narrator's own community can access it. Often, recordings of oral histories are placed in an open archive or repository. However, this part of the process also requires some thought. Certain subjects may be sensitive, and certain narrators might need to be protected. Narrators and their organizations might also have a stake in how and where the records are kept, and so might future researchers.

ORAL HISTORY AND MEMORY

When using the oral history methodology, a historian can compose a story from the oral histories given to them by the participants (narrators) they interview. This story will weave together individuals' experiences with the wider experiences of a community or society. But historians are never working alone in this meaning-making process. In fact, the narrators will already have constructed their own narratives from their memories. In other words, narrators do not just give the historian a random set of recollections. Rather, they themselves have already sorted and refined those memories over time. Thus the historian is usually not left with barely connected "facts," but rather with a narrative that has already been curated.

---

2 Irving Seidman, *Interviewing as Qualitative Research*, 4th ed. (Teachers College Press, 2013), 20–23.

In order to understand this process of curation, you might think about your own memories. There may be some you avoid because they are unpleasant. There may be other memories that turn into stories that you tell again and again, because you enjoy them—and you have found that audiences enjoy them too. Those memories may change a little bit every time you tell them. There may be memories that you forget for years and years, and then something—a smell, or a situation, or something you see on social media—wakes them up again.

Fundamentally, oral history relies on people's memories, and that creates a specific set of challenges. In order to understand these challenges, historians have to venture into the realm of the study of the mind. Psychologists, in particular, have a lot to tell us about **memory**. For our purposes, the research that matters the most focuses on two processes: encoding and retrieval.

Encoding is the act of putting something into our memory. Of course, we don't remember *everything*, and a lot of factors influence what our brain selects to encode. Some of these factors are evolutionary. Humans evolved to retain memories that would help us in our tasks, strengthen our relationships, and ensure our survival. Memories that seem particularly important to the memory-encoding parts of our brain are more likely to be stored. But there are many factors that can shape this process, such as the chemicals in our body, the environment in which an event occurs, our ability to understand what we are experiencing, and our relationship to the people with us at the time. These considerations all influence what we do and do not store.

Encoding is also a matter of perspective. We encode what we perceive, which might only be a portion of what is actually happening. That's one reason why eyewitness testimony is so notoriously unreliable—because everyone views only a small part of an actual situation, and from their own particular perspective. Similarly, because we miss many details when we are encoding, our mind will later try to fill in those details, which can lead to distortions and inaccuracies.[3]

Here are a few of the major points that psychologists make about memory:

- **Selectivity:** Just as people encode some memories and not others, only some memories are later retrievable. When we try to recall the past, our minds choose to call out some things that seem important, while others remain less accessible, even to ourselves.
- **Age:** You may think that age would automatically degrade memory. However, older people who do not have any particular cognitive dysfunction can remember things in the distant past quite well. This is probably because they retell these stories to themselves and others

---
3   See Daniel L. Bernstein, Veronika Nourkova, and Elizabeth F. Loftus, "From Individual Memories to Oral History," *Advances in Psychology Research* 2008 (54): 157–181.

often. For this reason, they are often better at making stories out of those memories than young people are.[4]
- **Setting:** As already discussed, the stories people tell in oral situations are greatly influenced by their specific settings and audience. This storytelling happens at the level of memory or within the space of a memory. In other words, people literally remember the past differently in different situations.[5]
- **Cues:** Part of the reason settings are important is that memory is often sparked by physical or emotional cues. Smells are particularly powerful, but so are other sensations like touch or sight or taste (think of your family's cooking). Physical objects and photographs can be important memory devices for this reason. But other cues include the questions you are asked and the conversations you might have had recently.

One other important topic to discuss, particularly when thinking about veterans, is **trauma**.[6] War is traumatic. Fear, death, and terror are all part of the experience of being in combat. Often, it represents an unremitting stress on the body and mind for days or months on end. But serving in the military—even without encountering combat—can already be enormously stressful, and in the case of this book, particularly as an African American member of a military that is just slowly emerging from Jim Crow racism. Many of the men we interviewed had undergone quite a lot of trauma. As we will discuss later, for some, it became a throughline for the narrative they told. Others clearly avoided talking about experiences that were particularly terrifying.

As far back as 1967, the researcher Ulric Neisser compared the process by which a person reconstructs their past to that of a paleontologist trying to put together dinosaur bones. They are essentially assembling a large collection of little pieces, some of which are missing, trying to make a story out of it. There is a lot of room for variability in this process, and the story that someone ends up telling may vary depending on their location, their audience, and even the way they are feeling that day.[7]

That does not mean we should think about oral histories as being either "inaccurate" or "accurate." Because of their high level of subjectivity, oral

---

4 Daniel L. Schacter, *Searching for Memory: The Brain, the Mind, and the Past* (Basic Books, 1996), 299–300.
5 Lawrence E. Sullivan, "Memory Distortion and Anamnesis: A View from the Human Sciences," in *Memory Distortion: How Minds, Brains, and Societies Reconstruct the Past*, ed. Daniel L. Schacter (Harvard University Press, 1995), 386–400.
6 Two important works that relate to this point are Kim Lacy Rogers, *Life and Death in the Delta: African American Narratives of Violence, Resilience, and Change* (Palgrave, 2005); and Alistair Thomson, "*Anzac Memories* Revisited: Trauma, Memory and Oral History," *Oral History Review* 41, no. 1 (Winter/Spring 2015): 1–29.
7 Ulric Neisser, *Cognitive Psychology* (Appleton-Century-Crofts, 1967), 285.

histories are indeed somewhat problematic as evidence of what actually happened in the past. However, it is possible for the historian to confirm that certain events truly happened, or to see that certain accounts align with the broader evidence. The team that worked on this book is fortunate to include a public historian, an academic historian, and a highly experienced Marine who has served for years as the historian of the National Montford Point Marine Association. That means that we can check and confirm certain elements of the narratives we are given.

But that's just a first step in working with oral history. A bigger step is to understand—and share with the public—the *messages* that are embedded in the veterans' narratives. In other words, we focus more on "what does this story mean to the narrator?" rather than "did this actually happen?" While we are *also* interested in accuracy, we believe that the way in which these men arrange their memories and the stories they choose to tell convey information that they think we and our audience need to know. So our main task is to try to understand and interpret those messages for you.

ORAL HISTORY AS A COMMUNITY ACT

So far we have dealt with memory and oral history as the acts of individuals. Remembering and talking about the past is also a public act, including for veterans such as the ones interviewed in this book. While many of our veterans have sometimes been reticent to discuss their experiences with their families or in public, they have over time created a huge body of oral accounts of the past. Moreover, they often hear each other's accounts, and talk about their experiences with each other. They also view the documentaries and read the written histories about their shared experiences. Because of this interaction and feedback, we can say that the veterans have a **collective memory**: a shared story of their Montford Point Marine experiences. This shared story may then also shape their individual memories over time.

None of this should be taken to mean that Montford Pointers (or any other community) agree on everything. In Part I, we show many examples where individual memories disagree about big issues and small details. But it may be that individual narrators come to tell their stories in ways that they think are acceptable or otherwise conform to the expected narrative of the Montford Point Marines. This process happens as the veterans tell their stories, both to each other and to other audiences, again and again. This may be why so many individual stories include certain key events that are told in the same way, with the same details. Some historians have shown how this kind of meaning-making can work in other communities. For example, Alistair Thompson works with memories of the ANZAC (Australian and New Zealand) soldiers who fought in the First World War. Using oral histories from across decades between the campaigns of 1915–1916 and the early 1990s, he has shown how the memories of veterans from this group became entangled with each other and also with themes that were portrayed in films like the Australian blockbuster war drama *Gallipoli* (1982).[8]

In many ways, oral histories such as this one are not only a study of the individual stories of the men we interview, but also of the way in which their collective memories are composed. As a result, we do not necessarily look at collective memory as a distortion, but rather as an act of meaning-making. Just like individuals sort through their own memories to tell a story, so too do communities like the Montford Point Marines sort through their individual stories to create a collective narrative, which may show some internal contradictions. So just like we seek to pass on to you the unique messages of individual veterans, we also try to understand and share a story that they collectively think is important.

How do we do that? Well, one important guide for us was the work of Nepia Mahuika.[9] A scholar and oral historian of the Ngati Porou people in Aotearoa New Zealand, Mahuika reminds us that oral history is not just a methodology for the researcher. It is also a practice that people do in their own communities. It is an active connection by which people recognize who they are and how they acknowledge each other. In order to be good oral historians who can effectively recognize the messages of our narrators, we therefore need to adopt some important practices. We must go in to an interview ready to learn. We must see narrators as collaborators on a project and not just as a source of information. We must give them some power over their work. We must recognize that they, as a community, have customs and protocols surrounding their ways of talking about their memories, and we must find ways to learn what they are—principally by "hanging out with" as well as "interviewing" them.[10] These guidelines are as useful for working with veteran communities as they are for working with Indigenous communities.

OUR APPROACH AND EXPERIENCES

Taking into account all of these elements, we developed an approach to the oral histories we were going to conduct. As described on page 10 of the graphic narrative, two of the authors, Rob Willis and Trevor Getz, had already met and proposed the project to First Sergeant Jack McDowell,

---

[8] Alistair Thomson, *Anzac Memories: Living with the Legend* (Oxford University Press, 1994).
[9] Nepia Mahuika, *Rethinking Oral History and Tradition: An Indigenous Perspective* (Oxford University Press, 2021).
[10] Mahuika, *Rethinking Oral Tradition*, 129–136.

who helped set the project in motion. But we knew we wanted to tell the stories of the Montford Point Marines as a group, as well as individuals. So we needed to engage the community of veterans in a way that helped to empower our narrators to tell their stories as authentically and comfortably as possible.

Fortunately, the National Montford Point Marine Association (NMPMA) existed to provide an institution and portal for setting up the interviews. Through a series of meetings and discussions, Rob and Trevor made an agreement with them to become partners in the project. In order to properly represent the organization, its former National President and current national historian, Master Gunnery Sergeant Joseph H. Geeter III, became a coauthor.

As is fitting of a collaboration, the NMPMA helped to select the oral history participants for the project. Two very active chapters—in Philadelphia 1 and Los Angeles 8—stepped up to help the authors make contact with potential interviewees. These chapters provided names of surviving original Montford Pointers in their regions, and the authors contacted all of these individuals. Unfortunately, matters of logistics and health complicated the process. One veteran, Captain Eddie Q. Hicks, was too sick to attend an interview. He passed away on August 22, 2023. An attempt to interview veterans in Washington, DC, was derailed at the last minute when the chosen facility declined to allow filming. The team then ran out of budget to conduct further interviews. But NMPMA partners had made sure that seven substantial interviews could take place in just a short period of time.

Partnering with the NMPMA brought a lot of other benefits to the project and to the narrators. The chapters of the organization we collaborated with are now mostly run by younger men and women who constantly provide support to the older veterans. These individuals agreed to accompany our narrators to the interviews, providing logistics and organization, familiar settings, and in many cases moral and ethical safeguards. Men and women like Major Brenda Threatt and Sergeant Major Charles Cook Jr. in Los Angeles and Sergeant Willis Gray and Mr. Odell Young in Philadelphia ended up playing pivotal roles in the process. Other narrators were accompanied by family members, like Carroll Braxton's daughter Monique and Jack McDowell's wife Brenda, who were invited to attend the interviews. Both of Sergeant Henry Wilcots's sons, Eric and David, were at his interview, although one had to join in late. In each of these cases, we ultimately decided to interview the veterans alone first, and then together with their family members.

Before the interviews began, we obtained signed consent from the narrators for the project. Together with our partners at the NMPMA, we carefully organized the settings (which are accurately represented in the graphic narrative). We also asked the narrators to bring objects or pictures. Sergeant Henry Johnson brought recordings of his voice performances. Gunnery Sergeant Roosevelt Farrow brought his wedding album. When possible, we asked about these images and objects as cues both to awaken the veterans' memories and understand their motivations.

We received help with recording these interviews from the Boeing Company, who provided us with a grant to fund a film crew to capture the oral histories in high-quality sound and video. We chose the crew carefully, because we knew their work would be important both to the interview process and to preserving the oral histories. Ultimately, we chose to work with El Dorado Films, led by Daniel Bernardi. Bernardi, an accomplished filmmaker who is also a veteran himself and leads the Veteran Documentary Film Corps, which has made many profiles and films on the experiences of servicemen and servicewomen both during their enlistment and as veterans. He and his crew travelled with us to gather the oral histories and participated in the interviews.

In preparation for the interviews, we developed a long list of questions. Ultimately, however, we found it possible to let most of the narrators lead us through their story for long periods. Many of them were well-practiced in telling their stories, mostly to local schools and news organizations, but also to each other. We knew we were going to have to take this practice into account in our analysis, because it meant that they had reworked these memories many times already.

In the process of interviewing, we were able to spend some time with and get to know the Montford Pointers' community. We were constantly impressed by their hospitality, especially in feeding a large crew of historians and filmmakers! We also formed some deep friendships that lasted beyond the initial interviews and helped us in our interpretation. In the months and years since the interviews, we have worked with the veterans to develop a number of short documentary films and helped some to write, edit, and self-publish their memoirs. We are also in constant contact to get their feedback on our work. Having Master Gunnery Sergeant Geeter as a coauthor is a big part of our relationship with the veterans and with the National Montford Point Marine Association.

After completing the interviews, we faced the difficult task of interpreting the narratives that our narrators gave us. Even after researching the full historical context and with all the help the NMPMA gave us, we found that we needed to carefully apply all of our interpretive skills and methods to help the veterans to tell their stories through a graphic narrative. In the next section, we will discuss what we learned about those experiences and will present our conclusions.

PART V
INTERPRETATION

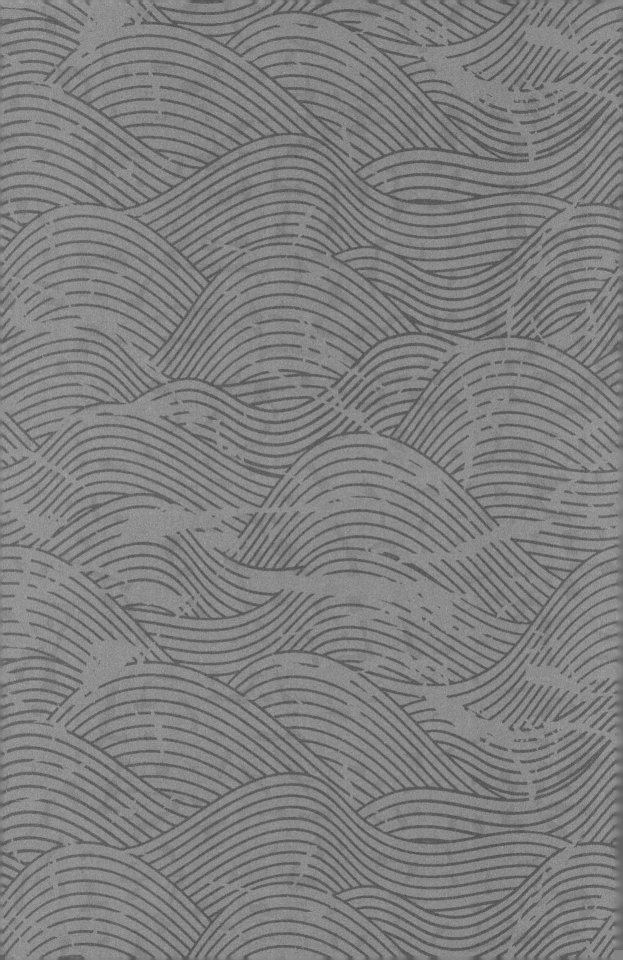

At some point in a research project, historians take the evidence they have collected and start to turn it into something that will be useful for others. This is the act that we call **interpretation**.

This process often overlaps with the collecting of information, but it also marks the culmination of the study. It is the step when the historian actually creates something out of the material they have gathered. Often, it marks a "convergence" of material. That means that the historian takes each piece of evidence and tries to relate it to other evidence. We see how and where the subject matter of oral histories, written sources, artifacts, and other types of sources intersects. Then we assess how each piece of evidence might cause us to confirm or alter our understanding of events and trends.

In the sections that follow, we describe how we interpreted the material we gathered through our oral histories in relation to other documents, images, and secondary sources. We begin by introducing the job of interpretation and the role of **critical analysis** before turning to two specific tasks: interpreting our sources to understand the collective experience of the veterans we interviewed and analyzing them to hear their individual voices. We reference many examples that you can find in the graphic narrative.

For most historians, interpretation results in a scholarly article or a book. In this case, we produced a graphic narrative. In general, the process was similar, but because comics communicate differently from written texts, we had some additional opportunities and constraints to consider. We discuss those in the last section of this part of the book.

WHAT IS THE JOB OF THE HISTORIAN IN INTERPRETATION?

Two of the most famous historians (if any historian can be said to be truly famous) are the Greek scholar Herodotus (484–425 BCE) and the German historical philosopher Leopold von Ranke (1795–1886). They described the job of the historian in similar ways. Herodotus called on the historian to retell the past *ton eonta*—meaning "as it was."[1] Von Ranke urged historians

---
1 Herodotus, *The Histories*, Book 1, Chapter 95.

to "tell the facts as they happened."[2] In other words, both demand concrete, factual, and accurate accounts of the past.

Historians generally agree that these are admirable goals, but they're not enough. The influential French historian Mark Bloch pointed out that trying to recreate the past is not only very difficult, but also often not the most useful pathway for a historian who wants to communicate what they have learned to others. You see, in order for history to be usable by people in the present, someone needs to help them to *understand* the past.[3] That's the historians' job at this point. The historian is not a passive vehicle for collecting and sorting evidence, but an active interpreter who helps an audience make meaning of people's experiences and actions, and the patterns of societies in the past.

Still, historians need to be very careful at this point. Interpretation is a process of weaving stories together from a large number and variety of sources and traces. It is impossible to tell the whole past from every perspective. This means that interpretation necessarily requires that historians leave some aspects out, that they connect some pieces of evidence with others, and that they make judgments in the construction of a cohesive narrative. It is easy for a historian to misuse their interpretation, to skew facts, and to try to impose lessons on their audience that do not match the facts. Most of the time, these are unconscious mistakes of a historian who is not paying enough attention to their responsibilities. Other times, they may be intentional distortions for ideological or political reasons. When these misreadings happen, the results can be problematic not only because they reflect the historian's view rather than the subjects' experiences, but also because they are usually inaccurate.

In *our* project, we committed to trying to avoid these mistakes. We wanted to make sure that we were answering the questions guiding this project accurately, but also in ways that would be meaningful to *you*, the people reading this book.

As we began to interpret the evidence to answer these questions, however, we found that our tasks in answering each question were slightly different. For example, take the first question:

- What were the experiences of the Montford Point Marines?

This question is all about "experiences." The answers we were searching for here were partly about discovering "what actually happened" (as Ranke and Herodotus demanded), but even more about listening to the

---

2 Leopold von Ranke, *Geschichten der romanischen und germanischen Völker von 1494 bis 1535 [Histories of the Roman and Germanic peoples 1494 to 1535]* (Duncker & Humblot, 1824).
3 Marc Bloch, *The Historian's Craft* (Knopf, 1954; Manchester University Press, 1952), 119.

oral histories of the men we interviewed to understand what they saw and heard and how they felt.

Now let's look at the second question.

- What do these experiences tell us about the military and American society during the Second World War?

The answers we were looking for here were less about individual experience and more about American society and global events during the period that our narrators were telling us about. This means that we had to intersect the narratives of individual veterans with a range of secondary sources and other evidence of Jim Crow America and World War II. By seeing how they fit together, our job was to craft a coherent narrative about these bigger stories.

Then there's the final question:

- What is the legacy of the Montford Point Marines, and what messages do they want to share with our society today?

This question doesn't really call on the historian to create a coherent narrative about the past at all. Instead, the main job of the historian in this case is to figure out precisely what the veteran thinks is important and meaningful and wants to share with you, and then to communicate it effectively.

In the sections that follow, we're going to talk through some of the ways we tried to answer each of these three questions.

CRITICAL ANALYSIS

As you can see, each of the three questions driving this research project required us to go about the task of interpreting the past somewhat differently from the other two. To answer them, we would need to make purposeful and thoughtful efforts to really understand all of the oral histories of the veterans, separately and together, as well as the historical context provided by all of the other materials we had consulted.

This job of diving deep into our sources—the oral histories—is sometimes called "critical analysis." This term can be misunderstood because the word "critical" is often used to mean looking at something in order to find faults and errors. But for historians, "critical analysis" instead means to examine something in a very detailed and thoughtful way. When we look at or listen to a source, we usually are not trying to figure out "*should* we believe this statement?" so much as "*how* should we understand this statement?"

Let us give you an example from our project. On page 97, we see an illustration of a story Carroll Braxton told us, with his own words in the speech balloons on the page. Braxton tells the story of two men who turned up in a training platoon in 1944 and asked to speak to him since he was the drill instructor. The men reported that they did not know they were coming to the camp, that their local sheriff had essentially forcibly conscripted them from a plantation in Mississippi, and that they had never even heard of the Marine Corps. On the next page, they report to Braxton that they did not even know that they were free—emancipated from slavery. Braxton, again in his own words, recalls the emotion that he felt at that moment, saying, "I almost cried when those two boys told me they were just learning they were free."

As historians, we had no doubt about the authenticity of those emotions or the significance of the episode. But we did have some differences of opinion about how to deal with the story. We describe these differences on the next page of the graphic narrative. The basic fact was that slavery had been abolished in the United States some eighty years before the Second World War. That's several generations. For Trevor, therefore, the story seemed more metaphorical than literal. It expressed how Jim Crow had preserved the terrible conditions of the slave era in many cases, even if not the institution of slavery itself. Braxton had told the story as part of a narrative about what it was like to be a drill instructor, a position thrust upon him rather than one he had desired. It followed a list of other men, illustrated on page 96, for whom Braxton had to show care and leadership as a DI. In other words, it was part of a longer explanation of the psychological damage done to Black men and the ways in which DIs like Braxton sought to be compassionate toward them.

Rob, however, took the story more literally. The episode triggered in him the known stories of Japanese soldiers who held out, individually, in the dense forests of the Philippine Islands as much as thirty or forty years after the Second World War had ended. It also spoke to his intuition, a gut feeling that this claim might just be literal and accurate.

"Intuition" is one form of reasoning that we turn to when seeking to understand our sources. It is an instinctive feeling that draws from our own experiences rather than conscious reasoning. There are other ways of knowing and reasoning. "Authority" is the power of a very credible or believable source. "Logic" is the appeal to conscious, purposeful reasoning about what does and does not make sense. "Evidence," of course, is the body of sources we have. Sometimes, these sources of knowledge contrast with each other.

In this case, there was not sufficient "evidence" to prove one way or another what these men had experienced, probably because there was a conscious attempt on the parts of powerful people to hide what was really going on at this time in rural Mississippi. We did, of course, try to see whether we could "converge" other kinds of evidence—written documents or secondary sources—to support or challenge Braxton's narrative. But we did not find anything suitable (although maybe another researcher can).

In the absence of sufficient additional evidence, therefore, Rob combined his "intuition" with the "authority" of Carroll Braxton, a deeply respectable and honorable veteran who is describing his experiences firsthand, to reach his judgment. Trevor, on the other hand, appealed to the "logic" of slavery having been formally abolished eighty years earlier. But keep in mind that neither of these two historians questions that Carroll Braxton legitimately remembers this event or that it was meaningful to him. Instead, the debate they had was over how to understand (and how to depict) this story.

In the end, as a team, we decided to begin by illustrating the story just as Braxton described it, but to then show Braxton himself as the key narrator, so that you can hear and see what we experienced as he related this episode. And we decided to dedicate part of a page to actually placing our two competing interpretations before you, the reader, so that you could decide.

This episode from Braxton's memory also has another meaning for us. It reflects the value of gathering a team of historians with different backgrounds and skills. Rob brought a deep engagement with the African American community, Trevor brought the methodologies of formal and public history, and Joe brought the extensive understanding of the Corps and the Montford Pointers from an insider's point of view. This combination gave us different insights and allowed each of us to make unique contributions to answering our research questions—and even our differences of opinions were usually productive.

NARRATIVE STRUCTURES AND SHARED EXPERIENCES

In a similar way, we learned far more from interviewing a number of veterans than we would have from speaking to a single person. And we do not just mean that we could get at different individual experiences. In terms of constructing a sense of the Montford Pointers' shared experiences, having several perspectives and combining them with other evidence allowed us to discover the key events, trends, and themes that made up the Montford Point Marine story and to sense how it can inform our understanding of the histories of the United States and the Second World War.

Building a shared history from many different interviews and sources requires some careful analysis. Historians often talk about how to do this analysis in terms of a set of discrete skills, and they have arrived at a set of terms that all start with the letter "C."[4] Our list is not quite the same as all other lists. Here are our five Cs.

---

[4] Thomas Andrews and Flannery Burke, "What Does It Mean to Think Historically?", *Perspectives on History*, January 2007, https://www.historians.org/research-and-publications/perspectives-on-history/january-2007/what-does-it-mean-to-think-historically.

- **Change over time:** What's the story here? Most historical studies have a beginning and an end, and they describe how some things have changed and others stayed the same. Sometimes, change happens for some people and not others. Centering the concept of change (and continuity) over time helps the historian to keep thinking about how to structure their narrative. For our story, we particularly look at the question of whether and how attitudes and experiences around race have changed in the experience of the veterans we interviewed. However, we are also interested in how they feel they have grown and matured as individuals.
- **Context:** The people we study exist in worlds and communities. Often, these are overlapping. People interact with these environments, are affected by them, and change or shape them in turn. In our case, the contexts that mattered the most were the camp at Montford Point itself, the Marine Corps, the US military, American society more generally, and the Pacific Theater during World War II. But it turns out that the communities and families of the veterans were also important contexts that helped us to develop interpretations about their lives and experiences.
- **Causality:** Historians often try to understand how exactly change happened, or what stopped it from happening. In other words, they want to understand the *causes* of important episodes, themes, and trends. In our case, causality was somewhat less important than focusing on experiences. However, we still needed to respond to such questions as how and why the Marine Corps began to accept Black recruits, how and why these were limited in their specializations and advancement, and how and why the veterans we interviewed came to hold the ideas and messages they wanted to share with us.
- **Contingency:** Establishing causality, however, comes with a challenge. It is an attempt to develop big explanations, when sometimes things happen for reasons that cannot easily be explained or do not apply in the same way to everyone. In other words, they have to do with very small, individual experiences and events. Because we are looking at individuals as well as bigger narratives, contingency turns out to be really important in giving full value to each veteran's perspectives and memories, and also in understanding why stories might be different even within a shared framework.
- **Convergence:** Even in understanding individual stories, however, historians often have to bring together many different sources and pieces of evidence. For us, the oral histories were the key evidence we used. But in order to understand them, we needed to support and extend them by looking at written sources, documents, books, and other narratives. So we would converge sources. In other words, we brought many sources together to see where each of them fit, where they raised questions

about each other that needed to be clarified, and where they could support our attempts to understand the oral histories. Convergence is even more important when trying to understand shared experiences.

All of these different skills supported our main analytic methodology, which was to listen and watch each of the interviews many times, taking notes along the way. These notes helped us to bring themes to the surface, and those themes helped us to construct our interpretation of their story and reach our conclusions. In constructing a shared history, we are particularly looking for the ways in which the oral accounts share memories. Some historians, like Steve Stern, call these shared moments "knots."[5] Such knots are useful for understanding how a community, like the Montford Point Marines, generally agrees upon its histories.

The best example of how we brought together evidence to understand shared experiences may be the structure of the graphic narrative itself. In listening to the veterans, we began to hear patterns to their stories. These patterns existed despite the differences in the dates when the veterans entered Montford Point, their time in combat or at war, and their choices after the Second World War. The patterns may have been shaped somewhat by the questions we asked, but the way the veterans answered those questions and the stories they chose to tell were more important in determining the ultimate structure. Often, the veterans used very similar words to tell some stories or introduce their personal experiences, indicating that they had shared their narratives with each other quite often. This sharing as a community formed those **memory knots** that would ultimately guide the graphic narrative.

Here are the knots we identified. You can compare them to the chapter structure of the book.

- **Knot 1:** How the Marine Corps came to accept African American recruits through the advocacy of African American leaders and the decision of President Franklin Delano Roosevelt.
- **Knot 2:** The recruits' personal decision to join the US Marine Corps.
- **Knot 3:** The journey to Montford Point, including (in many cases) experiencing formal Jim Crow segregation for the first time.
- **Knot 4:** The first day experience at Montford Point.
- **Knot 5:** Training at Montford Point, including the surrounding communities and the natural environment.
- **Knot 6:** The actions and personalities of the drill instructors.
- **Knot 7:** Service in the Pacific, usually punctuated by a personal story about fighting or its aftermath.

---

5   Steve J. Stern, *Remembering Pinochet's Chile: On the Eve of London 1998* (Duke University Press, 2006).

- **Knot 8:** Experiences after the Second World War, in particular the Korean War, and describing how the military or the United States has or has not changed over their lifetimes.
- **Knot 9:** Membership in the Montford Point Marine Association leading up to the awarding of the unit Congressional Gold Medal.

We chose to adopt this narrative structure for our graphic narrative because it seemed the most authentic and accurate to the stories the Marines told us, because it fit the context we had uncovered, because it told a story of change and continuity, and because it allowed us to effectively converge their individual experiences. As you will see, however, this does not mean that we flattened everything into one big story everyone agreed upon. Indeed, the individual narratives and messages of the veterans meant that there were often differences and even conflicts between their views. Let's turn now to exploring how we tried to hear those personal views and differences, and to bring them into the narrative in ways that would allow us to learn from them.

ANALYTICAL MOMENTS: HEARING INDIVIDUAL MESSAGES

One of the most important and difficult undertakings of our project was to hear the individual experiences and voices of each of the veterans whom we interviewed. Most of the secondary sources that made up our bibliography had done the opposite. Great historians like Ralph W. Donnelly and Cameron McCoy, whom we discussed in Part II, in the section on building a critical bibliography, have tried to collate the words of individual veterans to tell the stories of the whole group. But we saw value in also treating these men as individuals with messages for us. So we attempted to also understand what each veteran wanted us to know about their unique experiences.

There were surprises along the way. Gunnery Sergeant Roosevelt Farrow told us how much he enjoyed Montford Point. Raised in the North Carolina backwoods, he excelled at shooting and enjoyed getting three meals a day and spending time with his fellow recruits. He also showed up to his interview with his wedding album. Farrow was happy to talk to us about how he became a Marine, but also wanted us to know that he had lived a happy life with his wife of sixty-two years, who passed away. He impressed on us the importance of telling the story of how the Montford Point Marine Association brought the fellowship and friendship of the Corps to old men like him. This was not a message we all expected to hear.

There were also differences of perspective. All of our interviewees had African American drill instructors, and pretty much everyone agreed that they were tough. Men like Sergeant Major Gilbert "Hashmark" Johnson and Sergeant Major Edgar Huff are legendary and were mentioned by almost everyone we interviewed. However, they—and other early African American noncommissioned officers (NCOs)—could be demanding and even brutal. For some men, like Dave Culmer, the punishment they meted out was abusive. Culmer told us story after story about how he and others in his unit were treated by their drill instructors, and some of these stories appear in the graphic narrative at page 86 and 87. Culmer also told these stories at great volume and with frequent use of swear words, which you will encounter if you watch the video of his interview.

Now compare those pages to the stories from Master Gunnery Sergeant Caroll Braxton on pages 95–98. We interviewed Braxton in Philadelphia several weeks after hearing Culmer's stories. Braxton had become a drill instructor himself, although somewhat reluctantly. From him, you hear a very different view of the NCOs, leaders who cared for the men under their command very deeply indeed. How can we account for these differences? Were the DIs tough just because they knew the deck was stacked against these first Black Marines, and wanted them to train so hard that they would be better, stronger, and faster than the white Marines? That's the interpretation we heard from many of the veterans we interviewed. But there's no doubt that some men suffered a great deal as a result.

And of course, the veterans differed on the way they wanted us to talk about the role of race and racism in their experience. Certainly, they all had stories that made clear how big a role Jim Crow racism played in their time in the Marine Corps. From their difficult journeys to Montford Point Camp to being held back from specialist training and the terrible health and working conditions, they all gave plenty of details about how racism affected them. Underneath it all were the health and safety impacts of maltreatment and discrimination that Corpsman First Class Robert "Doc" Hammond told us about, described on pages 44–45.

Moreover, the nation's general failure to recognize their service continues to rankle today. Sergeant Henry Wilcots told us about recruiters turning up at his door long after his retirement. When asked about Montford Point, they told him that they had never heard of it. But most of the veterans did not want the impact of racism to dominate this story. When asked, off camera, how he wanted race to feature in the graphic narrative, First Sergeant Jack McDowell asked us not to focus on that "silliness." Instead, he suggested, we might tell a story of men who managed to survive and thrive *despite* discrimination. Jack's view has been influential in our interpretation, particularly because he was the genesis of this project. He is also the man selected by his peers to represent the whole body of them when they finally *were* recognized with the Congressional Gold Medal in 2013. We tried to stay true to his request to center the whole veteran rather than the experience of discrimination, while also honoring the individual views and stories of the other veterans.

INTERPRETING THROUGH COMICS: CHOICES AND DEBATES

The final interpretive choice that should be discussed here was the decision to represent these experiences and narratives—both collective and individual—in the form of a graphic narrative, also known as a comic.

Comics as a medium for representing the past lost favor in the United States in the 1950s, when authorities and parents began to see them as a conduit for immorality.[6] However, in other parts of the world, especially Japan and Europe, they were regarded as an important medium for discussing serious topics. Despite disapproval from some Americans, comics have remained popular throughout recent US history, but for a while they were carefully self-policed and self-censored. They were also seen as a medium that does not convey serious stories or messages, but is rather just amusements for kids. This began to change in 1992 when Art Spiegelman won the Pulitzer Prize for *Maus: A Survivor's Tale*, a graphic narrative about the Holocaust and its multigenerational legacy on survivors and their children.[7] Slowly, nonfiction comics began to emerge for the American market, and now there are hundreds covering historical narratives alone.

For us, comics provided three major advantages for interpreting and communicating the stories of the Montford Pointers. First, they include artistic, visual representations that are familiar to many young people today who read graphic novels, *manga*, Marvel and DC episodics, and other types of comics. Second, the visuality of comics is particularly powerful for helping readers to see and identify with human beings, more so probably than most text-only resources. But finally, comics give the author the ability to express meaning through art and design as well as text. Everything from the layout of the page to the lettering of the words to the images themselves communicates ideas in ways that are different from—and complementary to—words.[8] You can learn about the way comics communicate through a number of online guides.[9]

---

6   David Hadju, *The Ten-Cent Plague: The Great Comic-Book Scare and How it Changed America* (Picador, 2009).
7   Art Spiegelman, *Maus: A Survivor's Tale* (Pantheon, 1997).
8   See Nick Sousanis, *Unflattening* (Harvard University Press, 2015); Scott McCloud, *Understanding Comics: The Invisible Art* (Reinventing Comics, 1993).
9   Charis Loke and Max Loh, "The Word for World Is Image," *Singpowrimo*, December 10, 2020, https://www.singpowrimo.com/features/wordimage; Enrique Del Rey Cabero, Michael Goodrum, and Josean Morlesin Mellado, "How to Study Comics and Graphic Novels: A Graphic Introduction to Comic Studies," The Oxford Research Centre in the Humanities, https://www.torch.ox.ac.uk/how-to-study-comics-and-graphic-novels (accessed April 30, 2024); OER Project, "Three Close Reads for Graphic Bios," https://www.oerproject.com/OER-Materials/OER-Media/PDFs/Origins/Era1/Three-Close-Reads-for-Graphic-Bios-Introduction (accessed April 30, 2024).

Unfortunately, none of the three historians involved in this project are truly experts in making comics. Fortunately, our fourth author is: Liz Clarke is an award-winning artist, and it was through her that many of the important messages of this book came to be depicted through visual metaphors that speak as much as the text does.

In the very first two pages of the graphic narrative, we faced the challenge of depicting an elderly veteran in 2021 remembering the sights, feelings, and experiences of landing in the first invasion waves on Saipan Island in 1944. Guided by Liz, we tackled this challenge by showing Carroll Braxton split in half on one page, his modern face—with haunted eyes—overlooking the invasion in his memory in the next.

A comics page is an assembly and a narrative. As an assembly, it can contain all kinds of things set in different times and places. It can include original documents, paintings, and photographs juxtaposed with a historian (who may perhaps be sitting in their library or working in their car while the kids are at gymnastics practice). It can have a visualization of an interview and of an event that happened half a century or more beforehand. It can contain a map or a depiction of a microbe. And all of these pieces are arranged in sequence as a narrative, to tell a story.

Comics usually combine text and images, but some of our favorite pages in this comic don't need text at all. There's a tense and sleepless Jack McDowell on his first night at Montford Point on page 31, and there he is again on page 114, wandering through a nightmarish Nagasaki. The former page is dark and foreboding, while the latter is rough and chaotic. These decisions were made on purpose, to communicate feelings and sentiments that came through in Jack's voice and words during his interview. On page 110, art allows us to be humorous, showing Jack driving a truck into the ocean. On page 109, it allows us to be subversive, showing Black Marines in their support role holding up the more famous Marines who raised the American flag on Iwo Jima. Sometimes, these visual metaphors are quite literal, like the train track that separates two parts of the panel (and the town of Jacksonville, North Carolina) on page 27. Each of these depictions was a choice made by our team, and rendered by Liz, in order to reflect a message or story given to us by the veterans.

The answers to the three research questions that guide this book are there, in the graphic narrative. If you read the comic carefully and slowly, you'll pick up a lot of them. Of course, we also want *you* to be able to interpret the life stories of these veterans yourself. You can find some of the original video footage of the oral history interviews on which this book is based at firstblackmarines.org. If you listen to the veterans yourself, you may find that you have questions or even interpretations of your own. Feel free to share them with us by emailing us at tgetz@sfsu.edu.

PART VI
PRIMARY SOURCES

The oral histories of the veterans involved in this project are the main sources we used in our inquiry approach. These are available online at firstblackmarines.org. However, we also referred to a number of important written sources. These four are particularly important.

DOCUMENT 1
EXECUTIVE ORDER 8802. PROHIBITION OF DISCRIMINATION IN THE DEFENSE INDUSTRY (1941)

Reaffirming Policy Of Full Participation In The Defense Program By All Persons, Regardless Of Race, Creed, Color, Or National Origin, And Directing Certain Action In Furtherance Of Said Policy

June 25, 1941

WHEREAS it is the policy of the United States to encourage full participation in the national defense program by all citizens of the United States, regardless of race, creed, color, or national origin, in the firm belief that the democratic way of life within the Nation can be defended successfully only with the help and support of all groups within its borders; and

WHEREAS there is evidence that available and needed workers have been barred from employment in industries engaged in defense production solely because of consideration of race, creed, color, or national origin, to the detriment of workers' morale and of national unity:

NOW, THEREFORE, by virtue of the authority vested in me by the Constitution and the statutes, and as a prerequisite to the successful conduct of our national defense production effort, I do hereby reaffirm the policy of the United States that there shall be no discrimination in the employment of workers in defense industries or government because of race, creed, color, or national origin, and I do hereby declare that it is the duty of employers and of labor organizations, in furtherance of said policy and of this Order, to provide for the full and equitable participation of all workers in defense industries, without discrimination because of race, creed, color, or national origin;

And it is hereby ordered as follows:

1. All departments and agencies of the Government of the United States concerned with vocational and training programs for defense production shall take special measures appropriate to assure that such programs are administered without discrimination because of race, creed, color, or national origin;
2. All contracting agencies of the Government of the United States shall include in all defense contracts hereafter negotiated by them a provision obligating the contractor not to discriminate against any worker because of race, creed, color, or national origin;
3. There is established in the Office of Production Management a Committee on Fair Employment Practice, which shall consist of a Chairman and four other members to be appointed by the President. The Chairman and members of the Committee shall serve as such without compensation but shall be entitled to actual and necessary transportation, subsistence, and other expenses incidental to performance of their duties. The Committee shall receive and investigate complaints of discrimination in violation of the provisions of this Order and shall take appropriate steps to redress grievances which it finds to be valid. The Committee shall also recommend to the several departments and agencies of the Government of the United States and to the President all measures which may be deemed by it necessary or proper to effectuate the provisions of this Order.

Franklin D. Roosevelt

Source: Franklin Delano Roosevelt, Executive Order 8802: "Prohibition of Discrimination in the Defense Industry," June 25, 1941, Record Group 11: General Records of the United States Government, 1778–1992 (Washington, DC: US National Archives and Records Administration).

DOCUMENT 2
LETTER OF INSTRUCTION NO. 421 (1943)

HEADQUARTERS U.S. MARINE CORPS
WASHINGTON

May 14, 1943

LETTER OF INSTRUCTION NO. 421
CONFIDENTIAL

From: The Commandant, U. S. Marine Corps.
To: All Commanding Officers.
Subject: Colored Personnel.

Enclosure: (A) Copy of ltr CMC to Distribution List AO-3BO-Kb (0107743), dated 20 March 1943.

1. Enclosure (A) is forwarded for your information and guidance in connection with the handling of colored personnel.
2. The initial assignment of colored personnel to Marine Barracks and Marine Detachments at posts and stations within the continental limits of the United States will be in the rank of private first class and private.
3. While rapid promotion, when deserved, is necessary, it is essential that in no case shall there be colored noncommissioned officers senior to white men in the same unit, and desirable that few, if any, be of the same rank.
4. Subject to the above provision, promotion of colored personnel is authorized in the same manner as applicable to all Marines. In case where, for example, a colored corporal is qualified for promotion to sergeant prior to the time all white corporals in the unit have been replaced by colored ones, recommendations will be made to this Headquarters, and if the recommendation is approved, the man will be transferred to a post where his services can be utilized in the higher rank. The same procedure will be followed through all the ranks until only colored noncommissioned officers are employed in all colored units. The above does not apply to members of the Steward's Branch.
5. Beyond the continental limits of the United States, commanding officers will control promotions of colored personnel as necessary to carry out the spirit of the directive.
6. On all change sheets and strength reports, colored personnel will be shown separately. They will not be included in quotas for transfer unless transfer orders so state, except that beyond the continental limits of the United States they may be transferred in such manner as the Corps, Division, Wing, Area or Force Commander may direct.
7. Since the inclusion of colored personnel in Marine Corps organizations is a new departure, it is requested that commanding officers make a study of one situation as it exists from time to time and the problems involved, and make reports to the commandant, Marine Corps. This report should include the adaptation of Negroes to military discipline and guard duty, their attitude towards other personnel, and vice versa liberty facilities, recreation facilities, and any other matter that would be of interest to the Commandant.
8. All Marines are entitled to the same rights and privileges under Navy Regulations. The colored Marines have been carefully trained and indoctrinated. They can be expected to conduct themselves with propriety and become a credit to the Marine Corps. All men must be made to understand that it is their duty to guide and assist these men to conduct themselves properly, and to set them an example in conduct and deportment.

9. Commanding officers will see that all men are properly indoctrinated with the spirit of paragraph 8 above, particularly when Negro troops are serving in the vicinity.

T. HOLCOMB.

Source: Letter from the Commandant, US Marine Corps, to All Commanding Officers, dated May 14, 1943, Subject: Colored Personnel (formerly classified CONFIDENTIAL), Record Group 127: Records of the United States Marine Corps, History and Museums Division, PUBLICATION BACKGROUND FILES, "Brief History of Blacks in USMC, 1942–73," Draft Text & Source Documents, Box 134 (College Park, MD: US National Archives and Records Administration).

DOCUMENT 3
PITTSBURGH COURIER, "THE COURIER'S DOUBLE 'V' FOR A DOUBLE VICTORY CAMPAIGN GETS COUNTRY-WIDE SUPPORT" (1942)

Last week, without any public announcement or fanfare, the editors of The Courier introduced its war slogan—a double "V" for a double victory to colored America. We did this advisedly because we wanted to test the response and popularity of such a slogan with our readers. The response has been overwhelming. Our office has been inundated with hundreds of telegrams and letters of congratulations, proving that without any explanation, this slogan represents the true battle cry of colored America. This week we gratefully acknowledge this voluntary response and offer the following explanation: Americans all, are involved in a gigantic war effort to assure victory for the cause of freedom—the four freedoms that have been so nobly expressed by President Roosevelt and Prime Minister Churchill. We, as colored Americans, are determined to protect our country, our form of government and the freedoms which we cherish for ourselves and the rest of the world, therefore we have adopted the Double "V" war cry—victory over our enemies at home and victory over our enemies on the battlefields abroad. Thus in our fight for freedom we wage a two-pronged attack against our enslavers at home and those abroad who would enslave us. WE HAVE A STAKE IN THIS FIGHT . . . WE ARE AMERICANS, TOO!

Source: *Pittsburgh Courier*, Saturday, February 14, 1942, page 1.

DOCUMENT 4
H.R. 2447, AN ACT TO GRANT THE CONGRESSIONAL GOLD MEDAL TO THE MONTFORD POINT MARINES (2011)

One Hundred Twelfth Congress of the United States of America

AT THE FIRST SESSION

Begun and held at the City of Washington on Wednesday, the fifth day of January, two thousand and eleven

An Act

To grant the congressional gold medal to the Montford Point Marines.

Be it enacted by the Senate and House of Representatives of the United States of America in Congress assembled,

SECTION 1. FINDINGS.

Congress makes the following findings:

(1) On June 25, 1941, President Franklin D. Roosevelt issued Executive Order No. 8802 establishing the Fair Employment Practices Commission and opening the doors for the very first African-Americans to enlist in the United States Marine Corps.

(2) The first Black Marine recruits were trained at Camp Montford Point, near the New River in Jacksonville, North Carolina.

(3) On August 26, 1942, Howard P. Perry of Charlotte, North Carolina, was the first Black private to set foot on Montford Point.

(4) During April 1943 the first African-American Marine Drill Instructors took over as the senior Drill Instructors of the eight platoons then in training; the 16th Platoon (Edgar R. Huff), 17th (Thomas Brokaw), 18th (Charles E. Allen), 19th (Gilbert H. Johnson), 20th (Arnold R. Bostic), 21st (Mortimer A. Cox), 22nd (Edgar R. Davis, Jr.), and 23rd (George A. Jackson).

(5) Black Marines of the 8th Ammunition Company and the 36th Depot Company landed on the island of Iwo Jima on D-Day, February 19, 1945.

(6) The largest number of Black Marines to serve in combat during World War II took part in the seizure of Okinawa in the Ryuku Islands with some 2,000 Black Marines seeing action during the campaign.

(7) On November 10, 1945, the first African-American Marine, Frederick C. Branch, was commissioned as a second lieutenant at the Marine Corps Base in Quantico, Virginia.

(8) Overall 19,168 Blacks served in the Marine Corps in World War II.

(9) An enterprising group of men, including original Montford Pointer Master Sergeant Brooks E. Gray, planned a reunion of the Men of Montford Point, and on September 15, 1965, approximately 400 Montford Point Marines gathered at the Adelphi Hotel in Philadelphia, Pennsylvania, to lay the foundation for the Montford Point Marine Association Inc., 16 years after the closure of Montford Point as a training facility for Black recruits.

(10) Organized as a non-military, nonprofit entity, the Montford Point Marine Association's main mission is to preserve the legacy of the first Black Marines.

(11) Today the Montford Point Marine Association has 36 chapters throughout the United States.

(12) Many of these first Black Marines stayed in the Marine Corps like Sergeant Major Edgar R. Huff.
(13) Sergeant Major Huff was one of the very first recruits aboard Montford Point.
(14) Sergeant Major Huff was also the first African-American Sergeant Major and the first African-American Marine to retire with 30 years of service which included combat in three major wars, World War II, the Korean War, and the Vietnam War.
(15) During the Tet Offensive, Sergeant Major Huff was awarded the Bronze Star Medal with combat "V" for valor for saving the life of his radio operator.
(16) Another original Montford Pointer who saw extensive combat action in both the Korean War and the Vietnam War was Sergeant Major Louis Roundtree.
(17) Sergeant Major Roundtree was awarded the Silver Star Medal, four Bronze Star Medals, three Purple Hearts, and numerous other personal and unit awards for his service during these conflicts.
(18) On April 19, 1974, Montford Point was renamed Camp Johnson after legendary Montford Pointer Sergeant Major Gilbert "Hashmark" Johnson.
(19) The Montford Point Marine Association has several memorials in place to perpetuate the memory of the first African-American Marines and their accomplishments, including—
  (A) the Montford Point Marine Association Edgar R. Huff Memorial Scholarship which is offered annually through the Marine Corps Scholarship Foundation;
  (B) the Montford Point Museum located aboard Camp Johnson (Montford Point) in Jacksonville, North Carolina;
  (C) the Brooks Elbert Gray, Jr. Consolidated Academic Instruction Facility named in honor of original Montford Pointer and the Montford Point Marine Corps Association founder Master Gunnery Sergeant Gray. This facility was dedicated on 15 April 2005 aboard Camp Johnson, North Carolina; and
  (D) during July of 1997 Branch Hall, a building within the Officers Candidate School in Quantico, Virginia, was named in honor of Captain Frederick Branch.

SECTION 2. CONGRESSIONAL GOLD MEDAL.
(a) AWARD AUTHORIZED.—The Speaker of the House of Representatives and the President pro tempore of the Senate shall make appropriate arrangements for the award, on behalf of the Congress, of a single gold medal of appropriate design in honor of the Montford

Point Marines, collectively, in recognition of their personal sacrifice and service to their country.
(b) DESIGN AND STRIKING.—For the purposes of the award referred to in subsection (a), the Secretary of the Treasury (hereafter in this Act referred to as the "Secretary") shall strike the gold medal with suitable emblems, devices, and inscriptions, to be determined by the Secretary.

SECTION 3. DUPLICATE MEDALS.

Under such regulations as the Secretary may prescribe, the Secretary may strike and sell duplicates in bronze of the gold medal struck under section 2, at a price sufficient to cover the costs of the medals, including labor, materials, dies, use of machinery, and overhead expenses.

SECTION 4. NATIONAL MEDALS.

Medals struck pursuant to this Act are National medals for purposes of chapter 51 of title 31, United States Code.

SECTION 5. AUTHORIZATION OF APPROPRIATIONS; PROCEEDS OF SALE.

(a) AUTHORIZATION OF APPROPRIATIONS.—There is authorized to be charged against the United States Mint Public Enterprise Fund, an amount not to exceed $30,000 to pay for the cost of the medals authorized under section 2.
(b) PROCEEDS OF SALE.—Amounts received from the sale of duplicate bronze medals under section 3 shall be deposited in the United States Mint Public Enterprise Fund.

Speaker of the House of Representatives.
Vice President of the United States and
President of the Senate.

Source: Congress.gov. "Text - H.R.2447 - 112th Congress (2011–2012): To grant the congressional gold medal to the Montford Point Marines." November 23, 2011. https://www.congress.gov/bill/112th-congress/house-bill/2447/text/enr.

PART VII
QUESTIONS TO CONSIDER

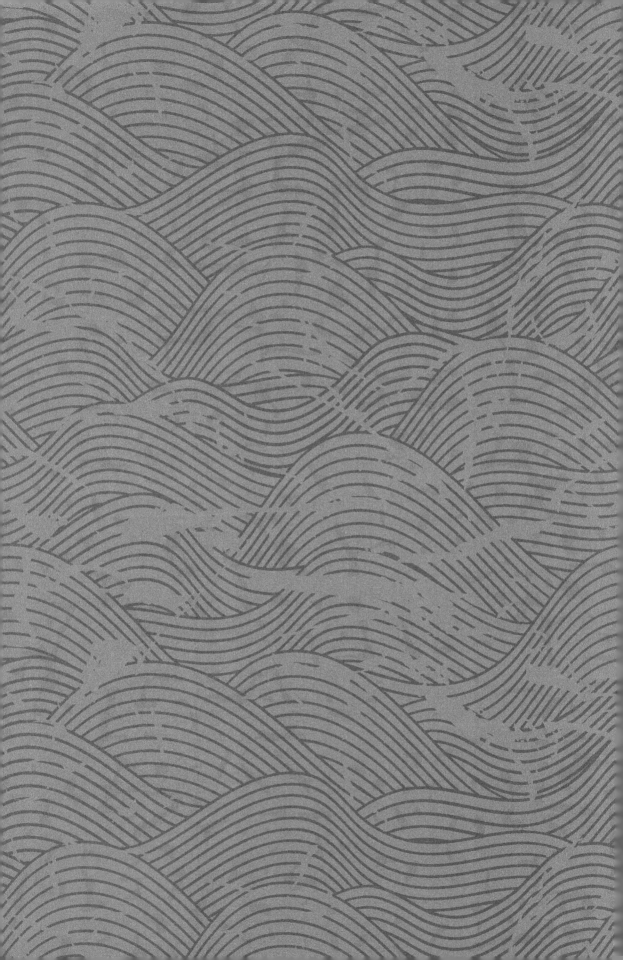

CONSTRUCTING A USABLE NARRATIVE

Drawing from both the graphic narrative and the historical context, the questions in this section should help you to fashion a version of the story of the Montford Point Marines that is usable to you.

1. What was Jim Crow, and why do the authors focus on it as a key context for understanding the experience of the Montford Pointers?
2. Who do you think should get credit for the promulgation of Executive Order 8802 in June 1941?
3. Why did the United States enter the Second World War?
4. What was the initial attitude of the leadership of the United States Marine Corps to the idea of accepting African Americans?
5. Why was Montford Point Camp formed, rather than training African American Marines in one of the two existing training camps?
6. What seem to have been the reasons, motives, or conditions that led some African Americans to enlist in the USMC between 1942 and 1949?
7. What was it like to be a "boot" at Montford Point Camp?
8. Who were the drill instructors who trained the Montford Pointers, and how did this change over time? How did the veterans interviewed in this project experience their interactions with these drill instructors?
9. What were the experiences of the first African American drill instructors at Montford Point?
10. What were the health and sanitary conditions for Montford Pointers, and how do we know about these?
11. What were the contributions of Montford Pointers to the Pacific Campaign?
12. To what extent did the Montford Pointers' service in the Pacific Campaign transform their treatment and experiences of racism? To what extent did experiences of racism continue into later generations?
13. What did the African American press, and Black intellectuals and leaders, think of the idea of African American military service during World War II?
14. What was the "Double V campaign"?

15. How did Montford Pointers and other African American service men and women contribute to the struggle against structural racism in the United States after the Second World War?
16. When and how did the United States government formally recognize the contributions of the Montford Point Marines?
17. When and why did veterans create the National Montford Point Marine Association?

EXAMINING MULTIPLE INTERPRETATIONS

18. Consider the team of authors. What does each of them bring to this project? What skills? What experiences and backgrounds? Does it matter who the authors are? Would different authors write this book differently?
19. Consider the veterans in this volume. Can you determine their motives from their stories? What messages did they want to put across? What messages did you receive?
20. How do the authors seem to answer the first research question: What were the experiences of the Montford Point Marines? Would you answer it differently?
21. How do the authors seem to answer the second research question: What do these experiences tell us about the military and American society during the Second World War? Would you answer it differently?
22. How do the authors seem to answer the third research question: What is the legacy of the Montford Point Marines, and what messages do they want to share with our society today? Would you answer it differently?
23. Why do you think the authors chose to begin the book with Master Gunnery Sergeant Carroll Braxton relating his experiences of landing on Saipan? How do the art and design on these two pages contribute to their goal?
24. On many pages in the graphic history, one or more of the historians appears inset in a box, drawn in a sketchy style. Why do you think the authors chose this style? How do historians "appear" (or disappear) in other history books they have written?
25. This is mainly a book about male veterans, but several women appear. What do you think of the way these women are depicted?
26. Read the text and look at the backgrounds behind each veteran on page 13. How do you think the historians chose what text to excerpt from each interview? How do you think they chose how to depict their origins visually? If you want, you can go to the videos attached to this project at firstblackmarines.org and evaluate their choices.

27. On page 18 and elsewhere, Staff Sergeant Dave Culmer uses a lot of swearing in relating his memories. What do you think of the way the historians chose to deal with these swearwords?
28. On page 27, a railroad track appears in the middle of the top row of panels. What do you think is the purpose of this track? Why do you think the authors chose to use this symbol?
29. Page 30 looks busy, with lots of panels and text, while page 31 has no words and only one large panel. Why do you think the authors made this design choice?
30. Consider the use of timelines and maps in the graphic history. How are they useful? Would you have made different design choices?
31. Page 37 is split in half, left and right. What argument or message do you think the authors were trying to convey? Do you think this artistic choice is effective?
32. Navy Corpsman First Class Robert "Doc" Hammond's story starts on page 43. He was technically not a Montford Point Marine, but he served alongside them. What does his narrative tell us about their experiences?
33. How did Gunnery Sergeant Roosevelt Farrow and Staff Sergeant Dave Culmer experience Montford Point differently? What do their different experiences tell you about the camp and about history?
34. What kinds of prejudice, discrimination, and violence did the Montford Point boots experience?
35. There's quite a bit of humor in the narratives told by some of the veterans, including Sergeant Henry Wilcots (see page 70) and First Sergeant William "Jack" McDowell (see pages 71–72 and pages 110–111. Why do you think they told humorous stories as part of their narratives? Why do you think the historians included these stories?
36. There was some debate about whether or not to include the ingredients of Master Gunnery Sergeant Joe Geeter's chili in the book on page 79. Why do you think the historians ended up including them?
37. Why do you think the historians used a visual metaphor of a smashed glass bottle on page 86? Is it effective?
38. What disagreement exists in this book over the role of the Black drill instructors? What different perspectives do Staff Sergeant Dave Culmer and Master Gunnery Sergeant Carroll Braxton offer on this debate?
39. Overall, the veterans told stories stretching from World War II to the Vietnam War and beyond. But most of this book focuses on the 1940s and on Montford Point Camp specifically. Why do you think the historians made this choice?
40. The image on page 109 is derived in part, and serves as a commentary on, a very famous image of the flag raising on Iwo Jima. What do you think the authors meant to demonstrate by including this image?

Do you think using an image here serves as effectively as a written argument?
41. Page 114 is visually quite different from every other page in this book. Why do you think this choice was made? What meaning does the art express?
42. The authors admit to purposefully choosing a less-than-flattering photographic model of Senator James O. Eastland on page 124. Would you critique this choice?
43. Are you surprised by the memory of the Korean conflict that stands out for Sergeant Henry Wilcots on page 126? What meaning do you derive from this narrative element?
44. How does the final page in the graphic history connect to the first pages? How would *you* have ended the graphic history?

CRITICALLY INVESTIGATING THE RESEARCH METHODOLOGY

45. Why and how do the authors distinguish between oral history as a method and oral history as a community act? Why is this distinction important?
46. How would you describe the guidelines for conducting an effective oral history interview or set of interviews?
47. What are some of the ethical issues connected to oral history collection, interpretation, and publication?
48. What arguments do the authors put forward about the way memory works? How do these factors influence the way we should think about oral histories?
49. In particular, how does trauma seem to affect memory?
50. Why was it important to the authors that they partner with the National Montford Point Marine Association? What do you think of this partnership model?
51. Why do you think the authors wanted each veteran to bring along a supportive family member or friend to their oral history interview?
52. What, in your words, is the job of "interpretation" for a historian? What should be the historians' goal? Consider the arguments of Marc Bloch, Herodotus, and Leopold von Ranke, but also include your own thoughts.
53. Consider the debate about Carroll Braxton's narrative of the two men from the Mississippi plantation. What are the positions of Trevor Getz and Robert Willis on this topic? What is your position?
54. Can you define or explain what it means to appeal to "logic," "intuition," "authority," or "evidence" in making a historical argument? Which of these do you think are most useful to historians?

55. Can you define or explain the five Cs of historical skills: "change over time," "context," "causality," "contingency," and "convergence"? What would you add or subtract in your own list, as an individual (or a class)?
56. What are memory "knots"? What "knots" do you see in this work that the authors may have missed?

ENGAGING WITH THE ORIGINAL VIDEO FOOTAGE

57. Watch one of the oral history videos of a Montford Point Marine veteran at firstblackmarines.org. Then consider how the authors portrayed that veteran in the book. Do you think they captured his message accurately? How would you have portrayed that veteran?
58. Find a clip from one of the oral histories that corresponds to an episode in the book. Now consider the oral history and the graphic history representation together. Do you think the representation—both visual and textual—captures the experiences accurately and effectively? How might you have interpreted this evidence differently?
59. Having watched at least one oral history video of a Montford Point Marine veteran, create an interpretation in a medium *other* than a graphic history—such as a podcast, a creative essay, a piece of art, or a nonfiction written historical interpretation. Then consider: How do the different features of the genre or medium you selected lead to different choices?
60. The authors made a choice to concentrate most of this book on the years during which Montford Point Camp was open (1942–1949), but the interviews cover the years that follow as well. There are many narratives within the interviews that are not represented in this book. Pick one, and create a historical interpretation of it. Try to be authentic and accurate to the voice and the message of the veteran. Then explain how you achieved these goals.

REFLECTING

61. Write a letter to one of the veterans. Tell them what their narrative means to you.
62. Write a letter to the authors. Engage with their choices. Tell them what was meaningful to you about their work, and what you might have changed in the book.
63. Consider an oral history project you might conduct. What questions would you devise? Who would you interview? What would your methodology be? How would you ensure that the narrators' message comes across?

GLOSSARY

BOOTS: A colloquial title given to fresh recruits by older Marines, especially prior to graduating "boot camp."

CIVIL RIGHTS MOVEMENT: Although the struggle for human and civil rights crosses many countries and time periods and continues today, this is the title normally given to the mass movement against racial discrimination and segregation in the United States stretching from the Second World War to the 1970s.

COLLECTIVE MEMORY: The process by which a group of people construct a sense of the past and their shared relationship to it based on a common identity.

CRITICAL ANALYSIS: The detailed and thoughtful examination of a body of evidence, using carefully selected theories and methods, in order to build an interpretation of their meaning.

CRITICAL BIBLIOGRAPHY: A method of building an understanding of a period, theme, topic, or group of people through the careful study of other people's work on this topic, which includes evaluating the origins, biases, meanings, and limitations of those sources.

DOUBLE V CAMPAIGN: The campaign, championed by the *Pittsburgh Courier*, to achieve victory over both the United States' enemies in the Second World War and over racial segregation and white supremacy within the country.

EUGENICS: The study of race, gender, and society, purportedly using scientific methods grounded in genetics, that has aimed at maintaining existing systems of power. Eugenics has resulted in discrimination and suffering for people with disabilities, minoritized racial and ethnic groups, women, and LGBTQ+ communities.

EXECUTIVE ORDER 8802: An order issued by President Franklin Delano Roosevelt in 1942 to ban some forms of discriminatory employment in federal agencies and ultimately within the branches of the military, including the US Marine Corps.

EXECUTIVE ORDER 9981: Issued by President Harry S. Truman in 1948, this order banned segregation in the United States Armed Forces and ultimately led to desegregated Marine Corps units.

INTERPRETATION: In the context of history, this is the process by which a historian analyzes and evaluates pieces of evidence and then puts them together in order to construct accounts that are accurate and meaningful.

INQUIRY MODEL: A general model that is adaptable for research at every level – from a classroom project to the largest professional scholarly pursuit.

HOMASOTE: A fiber-based wall board from which many of the buildings at Montford Point were made. It tends to degrade over time and has many limitations in terms of protection from the elements.

JIM CROW: A name for the system of racial segregation and discrimination that was in place in the United States from the end of Reconstruction until the 1960s. While it was more formalized in the southern states, it had implications across the country.

LETTER OF INSTRUCTION NO. 421: A confidential memo issued by Marine Corps Commandant General Holcomb in March 1943 aimed at limiting advancement opportunities and promotion for African American Marines.

MARCH ON WASHINGTON MOVEMENT: An organized movement, led in large part by the Brotherhood of Sleeping Car Porters union, to demand the end to discrimination and segregation in the defense industries and military in 1941.

MEMORY: For historians, a way of describing accounts based on the storage, retention, and retrieval of recollections of the past.

MEMORY KNOTS: One way of describing the shared ideas, themes, and events that emerge from groups of people remembering and describing the past over time.

NATIONAL ASSOCIATION FOR THE ADVANCEMENT OF COLORED PEOPLE: A leading civil rights organization founded in 1909, the NAACP played a key role in advocating for equality in employment, desegregation of the military, and the rights of serving men and women.

ORAL HISTORY: As a methodology, oral history focuses on the conduct of interviews and interpretation of testimony from narrators. Oral history is also, however, a way that individuals share memories with each other and their communities.

PACIFIC THEATER OF OPERATIONS: A US and Allied term for the area of operations against the Japanese Empire during the Second World War.

PORT CHICAGO DISASTER: In 1944, a deadly munitions explosion broke out in this California base, killing 320 troops, mostly African Americans, who had not been sufficiently trained and were not working in safe conditions. When many of the surviving soldiers refused to continue working in these conditions, they were charged with mutiny.

QUONSET: A prefabricated building made of corrugated metal that replaced many of the buildings at Montford Point Camp.

TRAUMA: An underrated factor in history, trauma is an emotional response to a terrible event and frequently features in veterans' experiences.